Yours in Friendship

an open letter to enquirers

by

Richard Allen

edited by Alison Leonard

QUAKER HOME SERVICE
• London •

First published October 1995
by
QUAKER HOME SERVICE

ISBN 0 85245 274 8

CONTENTS

Editor's Foreword

It was in 1982 that Richard Allen approached me to ask if I would be his "tutor" for a project of his: an open letter to enquirers about what he could only call "the Quaker Thing". It would, he said, not so much describe the Religious Society of Friends as examine the assumptions underlying its faith and practice.

I had known and admired Richard's writing for some years. I knew the unusual combination of analysis and profound understanding that characterised his style. I knew too that he had been instrumental in founding the Open Letter Movement, and had been closely involved with the Universalist group, the Seekers' Association and the Friends Inter-Faith group. His prime concern in his own meeting, Wandsworth, was for the enquirer. "Richard had the remarkable gift," Friends observed in an appreciation after his death, "of being able to reach a deep level during a first conversation with a new attender, and he always followed up the conversation with a letter or phone call..... Always a great talker, Richard was a good listener too, with a remarkable understanding of people, and many who turned to him with their problems were grateful for his perceptive and often down-to-earth advice."

What I did not fully appreciate at that time was the care that went into all Richard's writing. The final flowing style was reached by a process of drafting and re-drafting, of asking readers to offer suggestions and then revising it further, over and over and over. Wandsworth Friends again: "He always strove with scrupulous integrity to find the right word or expression for what he wanted to say." The result of this, and of poor health and the care of his wife Gladwyn in her last illness, was that the work proceeded slowly and was unfinished at his death.

I have included here all the finished material, plus tantalising extracts from the chapter on Quakers and Science, which exists in note form, much annotated and scribbled upon. Further chapters were to be on The Quaker Fellowship - organisation and methods;

Social Work ("not in itself the Quaker thing.... not equivocal on tangible moral issues.... Crime and punishment"); on Politics and the Environment (with Richard's involvement in green politics, this would have been particularly valuable); on the future of the Society of Friends; and on the consequences of following the Quaker way ("healing - suffering - death and after - wholeness").

Quaker Home Service have decided to publish Richard's work, despite its unfinished state, as it stood at his death. They asked me to edit and update it, as there have been social and political changes during the period Richard was writing, and since his death in 1990, which needed to be recognised.

Readers who are frustrated by the lack of Richard's later chapters can turn to other publications to fill the gaps: for instance, Harvey Gillman's *A Light that is Shining*[1] (a general introduction to Quakers) and Cecil Sharman's[2] and Barry Wilsher's[3] writings on the Quaker business method. Discussion on the future of the Society of Friends can be found in reports in *The Friend* in 1995 on the *Rediscovering Strengths* conferences around the country, and in *Leadings*, Chapter 29 of *Quaker Faith and Practice*. This last, revised during the period Richard was writing and published in 1995, is an invaluable source book, and Richard would have rejoiced in its appearance. Readers may also want to turn to Richard's other writings: *A Tender Hand* (Session's 1994) and *Silence and Speech* and *The QuakerWay* (QHS pamphlets).

No-one has quite matched Richard's ability to look beneath the everyday thought and practice of Friends and to articulate for the

---

[1] published by Quaker Home Service 1988.
[2] *Servant of the Meeting*, QHS 1983.
[3] *Quaker Organisation*, QHS 1986

newcomer the deep search and the paradox that lies there. The paradox is of a Society which values above all the voice of God - the "promptings of love and truth" - within the individual heart, yet at its best holds together in a disciplined community. Richard's insight into "the Quaker thing" is given in an early draft of the sub-headings to chapter three of this book:

Religious toleration essential to the Quaker thing.
Love is what really matters.
Love is impartial.
Love is non-attached.
Love is non-violent.
Love is unconditional.
In the end - personal responsibility and experience.

ALISON LEONARD
1995

viii

Dear Friend

If you have heard something of Quakers you may think they are a strange lot and wonder what makes them tick. Why do they sit in silence? Is their religion a kind of Christianity? Or a special religion of its own? Is it a religion at all? Are Quakers relevant today? And if so, are they just pacifists or peace-marchers? Or social do-gooders? Or what?

This letter is to help you to set about finding answers to such questions. I must add at once that it is not an attempt to convert you, but simply to provide you with information.

Letters, even open letters, are addressed to people. I wonder who you are, as I try to imagine you sitting here with me in my room? Of course you are a composite person: young, middle-aged or old; male or female; in a partnership or single; with or without family; rich, comfortably off or poor; of one race or another; of an intellectual, emotional or practical temperament; cheerful or harassed; of almost any conceivable occupation, or none that is outwardly defined; and with any imaginable life-history. I can't hope to make myself understood to all of you, but I shall assume that you are, so to speak, *looking for something.* And you are wondering if Quakers are worth exploring.

The problem of communication

This letter is not less personal because it is divided into sections with subheadings, and has a whole heap of notes and references and an index. I have provided these because the onus is on me - as it is on anyone who ventures to write on a serious subject - to use every resource of language and presentation to be clearly understood by the reader. This is very difficult, for the things that matter most can never be completely formulated intellectually or expressed in words. There is an element of mystery and paradox in everything as soon as you get below the surface.

This is particularly so with the Quaker thing, because it doesn't consist of propositions or principles or doctrines. It isn't a *thing* at all in the strict sense of the word. I use that slangy form of expression because every other word or phrase I could think of seemed to beg one or more of the fundamental questions you would be asking. The Quaker thing is nevertheless a very real fact of experience in the lives of Friends[1]; and like electricity, or the scent of a rose or the sound of a perfect fifth, it is not less effective because it can't be reduced to words.

I think the best I can do to help you explore the Quaker thing is to point towards it from different directions and describe some of its effects in the lives and conduct of Quakers. This will mean being rather repetitive, while at the same time having to leave some things in the air and take them up later on. I can only crave your patience for this. As John Donne wrote:

On a huge hill
Cragged and steep, Truth stands, and he that will
Reach her, about must and about must go.[2]

And however hard I try, I shall never quite succeed. One can't really learn about the Quaker thing from reading this letter, or any other writings. They can help up to a point; but you will need to attend a number of Meetings for Worship, ask questions of different Quakers, and go to any discussion groups you can find. Don't be put off if Friends give what appear at first to be vague and inconclusive answers to questions; they are all subject to the "intolerable wrestle with words and meanings"[3] that T.S.Eliot spoke of.

What the Quaker thing is not

Before I go any further I must try to disabuse you of some popular misconceptions about Quakers. (If you know a good deal already you can skip this section.) The main points to note are:

1. The Society of Friends is not a secret body. Quakers are delighted when people come to their meetings and want to explore their way.

2. It is also not a closed or hereditary body. Some Friends have been made members in childhood or brought to meeting by Quaker parents, but many people who have become convinced that the Quaker way is right for them have joined as adults, and these latter are now in the majority.

3. Without in any way criticising people whose religious search has taken them in other directions, the Society of Friends in Britain is not a body to which the terms "evangelical" or "pentecostal" could be applied. Nor is it a special interpretation of the Christian faith, or a philosophical theory or "-ism".

4. Quakers are not a strict puritanical sect which prohibits its members from drinking alcohol or using lipstick. Some Quakers are teetotal, others drink alcohol in moderation, and certainly some use make-up.

5. By the same token, Quakers are not a regimented, homogeneous group. If you get to know them you will soon discover that there is a wide diversity of opinion, temperament and practice among them. So please try not to be put off

exploring because one Quaker may convey the impression that Quakers are a strictly Christian sect, while another may make you wonder whether they are a collection of humanists; or because some Quakers sit down in front of Ministry of Defence vehicles while others think that sort of action is mistaken. This doesn't mean there is no common ground. The unspoken and unwritten thing that holds Quakers together is there all right, and if you explore patiently you will encounter it.

6. Finally on these negative points, and at the risk of upsetting some of my fellow Friends: the Quaker thing does not reside in what has been written about the origins and early history of the Society of Friends. Try as they may, historians cannot recreate and induce in us the actual climate of mind of past ages. Moreover, all religious groups tend to develop their special mythologies and extol their own special heroes and heroines, and in so doing slightly rewrite their own history. Quakers have also done this - though not to the point of making the Quaker movement into a cult of George Fox. All that can be said with any certainty is that the Society of Friends began in the religious and political ferment of the 17th century with a number of individuals drawn mainly from some rather disparate dissident groups but with certain insights in common. Since those days there has been an underlying continuity, a living tradition, which has successfully resisted the pressure of the surrounding religious and secular culture, while at the same time making a contribution to it.[4]

A living movement

Present day Quakers draw inspiration from the writings and the records of the lives of early Friends and others who have gone before - I shall quote from them myself - but if you are going to find the

Quaker thing worth exploring at all you will do so in the company of Quakers who are living now.

So I come back to asking myself how you come to be reading this letter. Through seeing one of the Society's advertisements? Through meeting a Friend at work? Or in a course of study? Or in connection with peace or social action? Or through a mention on radio or television? Or? Anyhow, it is the *inward* reasons that really matter. So I will now ponder a little over what seems to bring people towards the Quaker movement.

I
Starting Points

The Inward Nudge

JUDGING BY WHAT I have been told by a number of Friends, a common starting point on the journey towards the Quaker thing has been a sort of "inward nudge". This may come in response to some outward event, or apparently from nowhere. I think I can trace the beginning of my own search to a nudge of this kind. During a spell of unhappiness when I was about 23, I was fortunate to come across the *Reflections* of Marcus Aurelius. After saying that "life is a warfare and a stranger's sojourn" he goes on to say that what really enables us to carry on is

> ....keeping the daemon within.... free from violence and unharmed, superior to pains and pleasures, doing nothing without a purpose, nor yet falsely and with hypocrisy, not feeling the need of another man's doing or not doing anything.[5]

I can remember the very spot on which I stood when, after reading this, I suddenly found myself observing my wretched, hurt, angry ego, and looking at it as if it were an external object; and, inexplicably, feeling secure and at peace. In retrospect I suppose this was at first little more than a mentally healthy reaction to distress; but I soon began to realise that there was far more to the Stoic philosophy than a mere quest for personal invulnerability. So I began on a thirty year journey, with alternating outward and inward experience, that led me to the Quaker movement.

How far my experience is typical is impossible to say. We are all unique individuals, and we know very little of what is going on inside one another. Here is another Friend describing a crucial inward experience. Howard Collier, a doctor by profession, wrote:

> On a certain summer afternoon.... I came home after a long and tiring day and, sitting down in the shade of the garden, I fell into a brown study. Quite unexpectedly I began to talk to myself, and to my surprise, I heard myself saying to myself: "If you don't take care, you will end up by losing your soul." The humour of this remark struck me, since, so far as I was aware, I did not

believe at that time that I had a soul to lose. Looking back now I realise that that particular afternoon marked a turning point in my life.... This redirection of my search - from an outward search for truth in nature to an inward search for truth in myself - was the next step necessary for the healing of my own divided mind. [6]

Both Howard Collier's experience and my own contain elements which are common to many spiritual experiences. First, there is what the psychologist William James called "a sense of something wrong about us as we naturally stand" - not necessarily a sense of sin or guilt, but more of dissatisfaction, of having a network of contradictions running through our lives, of being deeply and fundamentally perplexed.

There is also the sense of having *two* selves - an ordinary thinking, feeling, busily practical ego, and another Self, a "knower" within us which looks at our ordinary self as if it were an external object. We look at our own perplexity from the outside, as it were.

I wonder if you have had any experiences like this? If so, you would not be alone. The Religious Experience Research Unit at Manchester College in Oxford has established that such experiences are quite common and happen to ordinary people.

The inward nudge may come, as I have said, in practically any outward circumstances. These may be adverse, even catastrophic: when a work situation becomes intolerable; or analysis shows that the tumour is malignant; when we have become estranged from someone we love; when the life of a near and dear one is threatened. Or it may come when for no special reason we feel a sense of inadequacy and failure, and our life seems pointless. But it may also come in a joyful moment: when we look into the sunset on a peaceful summer evening, or contemplate a beautiful painting, or hear great music. It may even come from nowhere, when we are sailing along in an uneventful calm and nothing in particular is happening to us. T.S.Eliot gives a hint of this sort of experience when he writes of

the unattended
Moment, the moment in and out of time,
The distraction fit, lost in a shaft of sunlight,
The wild thyme unseen, or the winter lightning
Or the waterfall, or music heard so deeply
That it is not heard at all, but you are the music
While the music lasts. [7]

The actual content of the experience varies enormously, but there is nearly always an inexpressible sense of direct knowledge of what lies below the surface of things; call it "the ground of being", "truth", or "God", or what you will - perhaps it is wiser not to name it. It is a sudden feeling that below all the muddle and petty division there is a unity in all things. Time as we know it ceases to exist; here and now is eternity. For a precious moment we are part of a miraculous whole. We are in perfect joy and freedom from fear. We are accepted. Sometimes this feeling amounts to what might be called "ecstasy". But more often than not there is no emotion in the ordinary sense; only a peace and a love that is beyond description.

I have gone on about this kind of experience because I suspect that, as with me, it was in one form or another the starting point for many people who are curious about the Quaker thing. But there are many other starting points - social, intellectual, religious - from which people have come to the Society of Friends.

Uncertainty

A common element in most fields of exploration seems to be uncertainty. During this century uncertainty has entered into science and politics as well as into religion. In the eyes of modern physicists, matter seems almost to have dissolved into systems of relationships and probabilities. In the living sciences Darwinian ideas about evolution, which have directly or indirectly dominated the minds of educated people since 1860, are now questioned, and among physicists hardly a month goes by without a new theory of matter.

In politics a more terrible kind of uncertainty has existed since the first nuclear bomb was exploded over Hiroshima: the possibility that the whole of humankind could be destroyed. The environmental crisis also threatens to engulf us, as pollutants enter the atmosphere and resources can no longer keep up with the developed world's demands.

In the religious sphere the traditional doctrines of the Christian faith are becoming more and more difficult for people to accept in the light of modern knowledge. And no-one can *make* themselves believe anything: if the mind lies down and refuses to obey, there is nothing that can be done about it.

What then can we believe? Now that it can no longer be taken that science and technology can fix anything and everything, there is at least room for humility, for a deeper reverence for life's mystery. But that means that the age-old questions present themselves more pressingly than ever. Life is an awe-inspiring business, with its strange mixture of dark and light, pleasure and pain, beauty and terror. What is it all about? The issues are growing sharper, the light and the shadow more starkly contrasted. Here am I, writing to you on my word processor in a rich London suburb where half the population is overweight, while thousands are dying every week of starvation in areas of Africa where women have to walk miles to fetch water. The Cold War is over, but news of devastating smaller wars, brought to us on television, prove to us in our comfortable sitting rooms that humankind has not learned about living together in harmony. What can we do about these overwhelming questions?

How do we find answers?

We all respond to these questions in different ways. Some people still hope for scientific solutions. They feel comforted when somebody can prove that these fearful things are caused by something else; the pain around the heart is not so worrying if the doctor says it is due to flatulence. From that point of view, looking into the dark background of one's own mind is dismissed as morbid introspection; it is far safer to get on with the job of living and stop worrying about the meaning and purpose of life. I went on like that for some years myself when I was studying physics. But when I came up against something that could not be coped with by sidetracking myself with work, I was forced to realise that this solution was no good for me.

Others find answers in a faith which provides them with beliefs which they can hold with complete certainty. For them, such a faith prevents puzzles and worries from arising in their minds. Let no-one despise a solution of that sort, for it is a great blessing to those who have found it. But for me, and I know for many people, it too does not work, and nobody can make it work for them.

However, there is another possibility. Some people feel moved to set out on a sort of inward journey. In a spirit of free and reverent enquiry they embark on a lifelong quest for a vision of truth or validity which will enable them to live as they are meant to live. They have no preconceived idea of what made them embark on the quest, or where the impulse came from. They might be described as seekers. Paradoxically they feel more secure on that uncertain quest than with any theory of certainty. Many, though not all, Quakers are in that position.

I wonder where, if anywhere, you see yourself in this picture? Attending a Quaker meeting for worship may have the effect, if it has no other, of helping you to find out whether this sort of quest is yours. So now I will say something about these meetings, because that is where the Quaker thing is present in a concentrated form.

II

A Quaker Meeting

How to explore a meeting

YOU MAY ASK: WHAT is the point of just sitting in silence with other people? There isn't really any verbal answer. The Quaker way does not lend itself to being directly taught; I can only give you some hints to help you to explore a Quaker meeting, and so find out for yourself.

You may, of course, have attended a meeting already; but if not you can usually find a Quaker group within reasonable distance from where you live. If it doesn't appear in the local telephone directory under Friend/s or Quaker/s you can get the address and the times of the regular meeting from Quaker Home Service, Friends House, Euston Road, London NW1 2BJ. Then try to attend a number of meetings. Every occasion is slightly different, and to gain a fair impression it is necessary to attend, say, five or six. If there are several Quaker meetings within your reach it would be worth while to visit two or three of them.

When you go to a meeting on a Sunday morning, or whenever it is, try if you possibly can to arrive in an unhurried way a few minutes before the stated time. There may be a doorkeeper who will indicate the meeting room. Just go in and sit down in silence; the meeting begins when the first person arrives. If you are early, please sit a little way away from the door, so as to leave room for latecomers.

It helps to settle down in a comfortable position - preferably with back erect, hands loosely in the lap and legs not crossed. Many people prefer to close their eyes. It often helps, too, to relax all parts of the body one by one, beginning with the feet and ending with the eyes and tongue, or vice versa. Then breathe deeply and slowly a few times. There is nothing magical or spiritual about these procedures; they are simply what others have found to be an effective preparation for entering into the silence.

'Centring down'

How does one make the journey inward? To be honest, nobody can really describe this in words. All I can do is to mention a few practical measures which Friends use to help them to "centre down". These are not psychological techniques or gimmicks, but well-tried, age-old disciplines to help people to attain inward quiet.

If you are a Christian, you can say over in your mind a short prayer which is of special significance to you - the shorter the better. Everyone will have a favourite. Often a single word, such as "God" or "love" repeated in the heart will help.

You don't have to be able to call yourself a Christian, however, to take part in a Quaker meeting. If you belong to another religion, you may also have a prayer which is especially dear to you. If you have no specific religion, or are one of those people to whom the eternal, "That Which Is", "God", or whatever name you do or do not use, comes in a more impersonal way, you may equally well recall a beautiful view or a favourite piece of music or poetry. We all have something precious on which we can steady our minds; for it is love that is the real gate to the inward pilgrim's way. Like "God" and "Christian", "love" is an overworked and misused word. What I mean by the word is: valuing something just for itself, being simply grateful that it exists. Love in that sense is specially there when we hold up other people in our mental arms and desire only their wellbeing. It can be strongly present in a Quaker meeting, where the members usually know and care for one another personally. It seldom fails to embrace the newcomer as well.

Difficulties and rewards

You may quickly find your way, but arriving at the still centre is a grace, a gift, which cannot be learnt or achieved or commanded; you can only open yourself to it. And that can be quite difficult. The Quaker thing is not a religious soft option! Sometimes the silence may seem cold and lifeless - a mere absence of sound. Or more likely you may find that, as soon as you try to centre down, distracting thoughts will dash around in your mind like bluebottles. Feeling sore about a tiff with someone, planning what to do next Thursday, wondering whether you turned off the oven - everything demands your attention. There is no cause to worry about these trivial thoughts or your inability to control them. Try to make friends with them, then gently put them aside. Then return to the prayer or other gate by which you entered the silence and start again. Even if that doesn't work there is no need to despair: if you do nothing but start again and again, you will find that the hour has not been wasted. You may well discover that a harassing problem has got nearer to being solved, or a deep worry about a dear one may have become more bearable.

Ministry

Sometimes the whole period of the meeting will be spent in silence, but more usually at intervals someone will rise and speak briefly. This "ministry" can vary widely in character. A speaker may refer to something which has happened to him or her during the week and draw some message from it. Or he or she may read a passage from the Bible or the anthology *Quaker Faith and Practice*. Occasionally somebody will offer extempore prayer.

Ministry is not at the level of ideas or argument. A meeting should never become a debate, and practically never does anyone speak more than once. What *is* said arises from the depths of what is *not*.

If you attend meetings regularly for some time, you may perhaps feel the call to speak yourself. It makes no difference that you are not a formal member of the Society of Friends; all present are on an equal footing in the silence, and everyone can give as well as receive. If the prompting does come, and refuses to go away, try not to quench it, however nervous you may feel. The right words will be given.

Sometimes you may find the ministry of others helpful to you on your inward journey - but not always. Friends try to receive one another's ministry in a loving spirit and refrain from criticism, either silently or in words. They remember that ministry that seems worthless or even offensive to one may be of immense help to another.

There is another point to bear in mind. The Quaker movement arose in a Christian background and has existed in it for 300 years; so it is natural that Quakers should express themselves in Christian terms, ideas and imagery. But many Friends have now found that they can also draw spiritual help and enlightenment from other religions, as well as from wise people of no specific religious affiliation; and this may be reflected in the ministry.

The gathered meeting

As the meeting proceeds, you will often - though not always - sense that the silence has somehow deepened; even the slightest restlessness has been stilled. For Christians, two of Jesus's promises are simultaneously fulfilled: "Where two or three are gathered together in my name, there am I in the midst of them"[8], and "Seek and ye shall find"[9]. An unspoken communion develops between those present and with God, however you conceive the divinity or the eternal. The "presence in the midst" has become a reality, and those who are aware of it have a sense not only of seeking, but also of being sought. You too may enter into that inward territory, where all images and thoughts, however lovely and sublime, fall away and you come into a pure stillness.

Every meeting is a unique spiritual adventure, beyond the reach of words. But this quotation from the seventeenth century Quaker Alexander Parker may convey something of the feel of what I have been trying to say:

> The first that enters into the place of your meeting... turn in thy mind to the light, and wait upon God singly, as if none were present but the Lord; and here thou art strong. Then the next that comes in, let them in simplicity of heart sit down and turn in to the same light, and wait in the spirit; and so all the rest coming in, in the fear of the Lord, sit down in pure stillness and silence of all flesh and wait in the light... (See *QF&P* 2.41)

Those that are brought to a pure still waiting upon God in the spirit are come nearer to the Lord than words are; for God is a spirit, and in the spirit is he worshipped.[10]

Children in the meeting

In most meetings of any size, Friends with children bring them to meetings for worship, and it is quite normal to find the children rushing about the Meeting House after the hour of worship. As it would be asking too much of most children to keep quiet for a whole hour, for all except about 10 minutes of the time they are taken to the children's room, where they have classes of their own. Some members of the meeting take these classes on a rota basis. In some meetings the children come into meeting for worship for the first ten minutes, in others they come in for the last. I think it is true for most Friends that the sounds the children make, and the little break when they go out or come in, do not disturb the silence but rather deepen the sense of fellowship and community within the meeting. If you have children yourself and want to bring them to meeting, it is a good idea to have a word with the convenor of the children's committee beforehand. Any of the other parents will introduce you to the right person.

Return to the world

A Quaker meeting usually lasts about an hour, but it is not fixed rigidly by the clock. One of the "elders", who look after the spiritual life of the meeting, will sense a gentle stirring as the silence thins, and will end the meeting by shaking hands with someone near them, often another elder or the "clerk" (secretary) of the meeting. This is often followed by a general shaking of hands all round. The clerk then reads out notices about events in the coming week, information about other meetings, conferences etc.

After meeting, coffee and tea are usually served and there is an opportunity to talk with Friends, ask questions and look at books and leaflets about the Society. As those present gradually drift away, you may experience what Alexander Parker meant when he went on to write:

> In such a meeting there will be an unwillingness to part asunder, being ready to say in yourselves, it is good to be here.[11]

III

What do Quakers Believe ?

WHEN SO LITTLE is said in Quaker meetings, you may wonder whether Quakers have any definite religious beliefs. Even if the Quaker thing itself can't be expressed in words, doesn't it have at least some effect on what Quakers think? And if so, isn't there *something* they could say about this - not merely in an intellectual way, because what we are all looking for is not a set of notions, but something to believe in that we "feel in our bones" is true and reliable?

But how can we know what is really true? What tests or standards can we apply? The basic question is: where do we look for *authority?* Do Quakers think that by just sitting there together they can find out absolute truth about themselves and the world? And with nobody to instruct them, won't the 18,000 plus Quakers in Britain have 18,000 different religions with 18,000 different gods? This may seem to you to be an insoluble puzzle, especially if you have grown up in a religious background where it is taken for granted that people can, and should, rely on some objective source of authority outside themselves.

Many people do rely on external authority. But then how do they know that the authority they have chosen is in fact reliable? And, more basically, is there anything at all outside of ourselves that we can get in touch with? When we think or reflect or pray, are we only looking at our own thoughts - which may in turn be only by-products of electrical and chemical events in our brains? Does something divine (whatever you may call it) apart from our own thoughts and feelings really exist? If it does, is it there in its own right, independent of us? Or is it not out there, but in here, in us, and is the process of finding it no more than encountering part of ourselves? Or is it both here and there?

People have puzzled over these questions since the beginning of recorded time. They are not just academic exercises for philosophers; for the answers, if any, determine what we think we are in the world for, and what we are to do with our lives. Much of what I am now going to write will be a rather discursive search for some answers.

It is difficult to know where to start. The Quaker movement has existed for over 300 years in a country in which the observances of the Christian faith have, until quite recently, been part and parcel of the life of the majority of people. That is no longer the case, but the fact remains that the Quaker thing appeared in a strictly Christian context, and its language and thought patterns are still strongly Christian. Now this presents me with a dilemma. You may already be a Christian yourself, in some sense of that wide and vague expression; but you may equally likely regard yourself as an agnostic or atheist, or belong to another faith altogether. You may even be actively against Christianity because of what you have read of its history or have experienced in the conduct of people who call themselves Christian. This doesn't necessarily mean that the Quaker thing is irrelevant to you. I will come back later to the question of how far it is confined to the Christian context or extends outside it. All I want to do here is to repeat that I am not trying to convert you. I have to start somewhere, and for a person living in Britain the Christian faith is still the natural starting point.

I will therefore now look at the main sources to which people have looked for authority in the Christian field. I should warn you, however, that for reasons which will only emerge gradually, most Quaker ideas start with negatives, though they work up to a positive conclusion. This paradox is encountered again and again as you try to get to the heart of the Quaker thing. I don't apologise for this; life itself is paradoxical - as you may have already discovered.

The Bible not the final authority

For most of us the obvious source of authority in religious matters is the Bible, so I will start there. But I realise that to some people - and you may be one of them - the Bible is not merely a record of the life and teachings of the founder of Christianity, but the inspired word of God and the sole source of ultimate truth. I don't know where you stand on this, and I am anxious not to cause you distress, but in recent years certain facts about the Judaeo-Christian Bible have gradually become public knowledge, and one cannot decide how much authority to ascribe to the Bible without looking those facts in the face.

It still isn't easy to get to the bottom of this matter, but here is a broad summary of the facts as far as I, as a non-scholar, have been able to discover them for myself:

1. There is no original manuscript of any Biblical writing. For the general public in Britain today the Bible is an English translation - or rather a number of slightly differing translations - prepared by scholars from copies of the originals. Apart from some fragments of earlier date, the very earliest of these copies are from the fourth century after Jesus's life, and many are much later.

2. In many places the texts of the copies are obscure or conflict with one another, and the translators have had to adopt what they guessed to be the most probable readings. A glance at the footnotes in the New English Bible will give you some idea of the extent of these uncertainties.

3. There is wide agreement among scholars that the earliest books of the New Testament to have been composed were the letters of Paul of Tarsus to the Christian groups in Rome and Corinth. These were probably written around 40 CE - that is, within a decade or two after the death of Jesus of Nazareth.

4. The Gospels - which to the plain person are the most important of the New Testament books, because they are a record of what Jesus said and give some account of his birth, life and death - were composed at least 30 years after the events they describe. The Gospel of John is probably later still.

5. On linguistic grounds alone it is unlikely that we can have a wholly accurate record of what was actually said or written. The reasons are:

(a) Jesus must have spoken Aramaic, a now-dead language allied to Hebrew; but the Gospels were composed in Greek and were therefore already in effect a translation. The manuscripts of the New Testament are either in Greek or in further translations into Latin. This means that Jesus's words in the English texts have undergone two or even three translations on their way to the present-day reader.

(b) Although a vast amount of study has been put into Latin and New Testament Greek, they are dead languages, and nobody can know exactly what they conveyed to those who actually used them. This applies particularly to abstract words like "logos", which seems to occur in nearly a dozen different senses. Sometimes a word occurs only once and translators have had to deduce the probable meaning of the original from the context - an exceedingly hazardous procedure, as I, a professional translator working from a living language, am only too well aware.

(c) Even if the exact meaning of the manuscript could be ascertained, it could not be fully and precisely rendered in English. No translation can ever be perfect. No professional translator would venture to claim to having made a perfect translation between two living languages; and it is far more difficult still to render the meaning of writings in dead languages into the living language of a different culture many centuries later.

(d) These difficulties apply with at least equal force to the ancient Hebrew documents of the Old Testament, which after all makes up three-quarters of the whole Bible.

6. There is no independent contemporary account of the life of Jesus. Practically the only sources of information are the Gospels and a few references elsewhere in the New Testament. Some apocryphal books have been discovered, but they are almost certainly of even later date than the canonical Gospels

(ie. those ultimately accepted as authoritative by the Christian church). There are brief references to Jesus and a good deal about the early Christian church in the works of the Jewish historian Josephus, who was born around 37 AD (ie. about 4 years after the death of Jesus) and wrote during the period 70 to 95 AD; but his writings are also only available in copies which most scholars agree were edited in the course of copying - mainly by Christians.

7. To sum up: any English-speaking person who relies for authority on the words of the Bible is tacitly assuming that the creator of the world decided to communicate real and unshakeable truth about himself to his creatures through a person who died 2,000 years ago, who wrote nothing, and whose life and teachings are now contained in English translations from imperfect manuscripts written in dead languages, which in turn are copies (made four centuries or so later) of lost originals which were for the most part in effect translations from other languages now dead, were composed mainly at least a generation or more after the events they describe, and about whose exact meaning and significance scholars have been arguing inconclusively for centuries.

To ordinary common sense people these facts are puzzling, and may make them sceptical of the whole Christian setup. To members of the Christian churches they can be deeply disturbing, because they call in question the most important basis of authority of the churches, especially Protestant ones. The Christian scheme of things owes its validity to what purport to be historical facts, and if the sources of knowledge of those facts are questioned there is bound to be anxiety. It is therefore only natural that scholars committed to the Christian faith should have been careful not to say anything that they felt would undermine the faith by which ordinary Christians lived; and they seem to have maintained until recently a sort of conspiracy of silence on the whole subject. With the publication and wide sales of John Robinson's *Honest to God,* Don Cupitt's *The Sea of Faith* and other popular works, the real status of the scriptures has gradually become known to the general public.

But the Bible and other writings can help

After what I have said you may wonder whether the Bible carries any weight at all with Quakers. The answer is that many Friends do value it, though in their own characteristic way. The whole question of the significance of religious writings is more subtle and complicated than it looks at first sight. All serious writers about the great mysteries of life must have had a strong urge to communicate, and those who now read what they wrote must do so in the hope of learning something; but what the reading process really amounts to is one of the secrets of the human psyche. In a fuzzy and overlapping way people seem to approach words in the religious context from four different points of view, each associated with a quite different idea of what religious language is for:

(1) People of a generally intellectual turn of mind naturally seek truth primarily by study. Both writers and readers of that disposition work on the assumption that, if you try hard enough, truth can be reduced to verbal propositions. At their best, those who write from that standpoint have sought to express themselves in cool, precise terms with fairness, courtesy and a wealth of knowledge. Shining examples are Catholic theologians like Rahner, and among Protestants the late John Robinson.[12]

(2) People to whom feeling is vitally important are drawn more to writings of an evangelical kind, where the writers try with passionate conviction to induce in the reader a feeling that will cause the "penny to drop". The aim is the conversion of readers, to their eternal benefit in this life and in life after death. This subject is explored in Ian Ramsey's *Religious Language*[13] and writing of this kind can be found in many religious bookshops.

(3) For other people, drama, ritual, music and poetry are specially important means for getting hold of truth. Such people find help and instruction in hymns and anthems and in such books as the Anglican Book of Common Prayer, as well as in the rituals themselves. For such people language is essentially a gateway to devotional exercises which are part of the fabric of their lives.

(4) Finally, there is a kind of religious writing in which the writers are trying to say something that they know can never be fully expressed in words. In their struggles to do so they resort to strange metaphors, parables, riddles and paradoxes; though even so, words "strain, crack and sometimes break under the burden"[14]. The best they can do is to point towards their experience and hope that their readers will recognise it in themselves. Examples of this sort of writing occur in the Christian tradition in the works of such writers as the unknown author of *The Cloud of Unknowing* and Mother Julian of Norwich, and in the poetry of John Donne and T.S.Eliot.

Much of Friends' writings fall into this category. Perhaps significantly, they have built up over the past 300 years a "Book of Discipline" which is not a book of rules but an anthology of short extracts from writings by and about Friends who have gone before or are living now. This book, *Quaker Faith and Practice*, is the principal source of help for Friends, as its predecessor *Christian Faith and Practice in the Experience of the Religious Society of Friends* was for the previous generation. It is essential reading if and when you feel like exploring the Quaker thing in any depth.

We can never really know what goes on within other people as they read, and how what they read "works" (or fails to work) for them. Even if I knew you personally, I could not fully enter into your experience. We can't even be quite sure that we understand our own inner processes. I suspect that, on the all-important question of authority, writers in the four categories work on their readers in different ways. For my own part, after half a century I can clearly recall the deep impression that Marcus Aurelius's *Reflections* made on me. As I read, something suddenly clicked into place. But this was not a conversion experience. The author did not appear as someone armed with an external authority that I was bound to obey: he confirmed convincingly some insights that were already beginning to form within me. I felt that he was an exceptionally wise mentor whose advice I could safely follow, but I did not feel that he was a divine person, or that he was inspired by God - indeed at that time I was resistant to religion of any sort.

Since then I have come across other writings, both Christian and non-Christian, which have helped me forward in the same sort of way; and I suspect that this is true of many other Friends. Finding our ideas reflected in the writings of the saints and sages is not *proof* that we are on the right track, but we are at least in worthy company.

What part then does the Judaeo-Christian Bible play in the reading of Friends? What real authority, if any, does it have for them? The answer depends a great deal on what part of the Bible you are referring to. It is in fact a library of books with a great diversity of style, language and content. There is theological writing, especially in the letters of Paul of Tarsus; historical and quasi-historical material in the Jewish part of the volume; rhetoric in the Old Testament prophets; and poetry in the Psalms. Writing in the fourth category is relatively rare in the New Testament, but it does appear in the parables and sayings attributed to Jesus of Nazareth, especially in John's gospel. The letter of James also contains writing which rings a bell with many Friends.

In reading the Bible, or any other writings, Friends have always worked on two principles: (a) they have avoided taking the texts in a narrow, literal way, and have tried to enter into the spirit in which the writers stood when they were writing; and (b) they have then looked to see whether what they have understood of the writers' meaning was valid for themselves. It was Friends' own experience that really counted - and this often came first. After writing of his own experience,

George Fox added: "This I saw in the pure openings of the Light, without the help of any man, neither did I then know where to find it in the scriptures, though afterwards, searching the scripture I found it."[15] In short, the real value to Friends of the Bible and all other scriptural writings lies in confirming insights which are already germinating within them.

It is remarkable that the early Quakers should have developed this approach when they were under such great pressure, external and internal, from the strange mixture of theological disputation, political unrest and sheer superstition that dominated the age in which they lived. But they did. The status of the Bible was made explicit by their theologian, Robert Barclay: after saying in effect that he accepted the scriptures as historically correct and a "full and ample account" of Christian doctrine, he went on: "Nevertheless, because they are only a declaration of the fountain and not the fountain itself, therefore they are not to be esteemed the principal ground of all truth and knowledge, nor yet the adequate or primary rule of faith and manners." They are "a secondary rule, subordinate to the Spirit, from which they have all their excellency and certainty." [16]

To sum up, for most Friends the Bible is valued because of the way in which, together with other writings, it helps us to find answers within ourselves. We don't sell out to it, but equally we don't merely pick out just the passages that support our own pet ideas. We try to receive the words into our inmost hearts and then make up our own minds. As George Fox said at an early stage in his career: "You will say, Christ saith this, and the apostles say this; but what canst thou say?"[17]

In the end, words and writings are not the final source of authority. As Isaac Penington put it:

"... the end of words is to bring men to the knowledge of things beyond what words can utter. So learn of the Lord to make a right use of the Scriptures: which is by esteeming them in their right place, and prizing that above them which is above them." [18]

For my own part, I have profited much from what wise ones, both Quakers and others, have written in the past, and I have acknowledged my debt by quoting them freely in this letter. But I am not pressing you to accept what they say - or what I say with their assistance - as having some magical property that makes it unassailable truth. If you pick up some of the Quaker thing by reading this letter it is simply because I have expressed some ideas which you have felt disposed to make your own.

Avoidance of creeds and dogmas

So far as can be seen from the Bible, Jesus did not lay down any formal statements to encapsulate his teaching; nor did the first Christians. As the new religion grew, short definitions of essentials seem to have been evolved gradually to help newcomers. But when the movement became large and powerful and was adopted by states as an official religion, authoritative statements of its basic principles became politically as well as spiritually necessary. The state had to settle the right view of certain essentials, in particular the exact status of Jesus: whether he was God or man, or both, and if both, how the two elements or aspects were related. After a great deal of argument, some of it deplorably bitter, the present creeds became fixed about the fifth century AD and have remained unchanged to this day.

The practical effect of the creeds was to put a ring fence round the Christian faith, distinguishing those who were "in" from those who were "out". In addition, the Christian church developed over the centuries a body of doctrine, including certain dogmas - that is, definitions of what the church regarded as truths revealed to it by God.

It cannot be concealed that the development of the creeds and dogmas was accompanied by controversies, divisions and persecution in a spirit far removed from that of the Jesus portrayed in the Gospels; and some of these divisions still exist. More seriously still, during the past 300 years, and at a steadily increasing rate since the last war, many churchgoers have found that there are items in the creeds, such as the virgin birth of Jesus, which they just can't bring themselves to believe. They may even have doubts about whether he was, at any rate in any physical sense, raised from the dead. So they find themselves solemnly declaring every time they go to church that they believe things which in fact they do not really believe. Some loyally and patiently accept this situation as part of the price of belonging to the fellowship of their church. They often take a humble view of their ability or even their right to question established doctrines, and they may feel a sense of guilt at their unbelief. But those who are scrupulous about intellectual integrity begin to wonder whether they can properly go on belonging to their churches. They may also feel under pressure from those members of the congregation who do believe what is in the creeds. In Britain, the Christian churches are in a deepening crisis of belief.

There is a wide range of belief - and disbelief - among Quakers too. Some are in positions not far removed from adherence to the official doctrines of the Christian churches, but others are probably a long way from them. This diversity alone makes the avoidance of creeds and dogmas essential to the Society of Friends. But the matter goes much deeper than that. It is not just that beliefs are difficult to define in words, but that the things that really matter to Friends are in a region altogether "beyond what words can utter". It is not so much the content of the creeds that troubles Friends, but the attempt to use words to fix what cannot by its nature be expressed in words at all. The use of a creed cannot be reconciled with the continuous search for guidance in life and in the silent meeting for worship. Friends have always recognised that, for them, the following of a religion could never be something static. Whatever else may be said about history, it certainly changes and moves on. Certain basic truths about human life are eternal, but our apprehension of them grows and our expression of them changes.

The Society of Friends does not impose any clear-cut test of belief on its members. There is a part of *Quaker Faith and Practice* (which is also published separately) called *Advices and Queries*, which is intended to recall Friends' minds to essentials. But it is not a creed or definitive statement; in fact *Advices and Queries*, like the anthology in which it is included, is a publication that is revised and renewed in each generation. As early as 1656 some Friends wrote words which are given as a reminder at the beginning:

> Dearly beloved Friends, these things we do not lay upon you as a rule or form to walk by, but that all, with the measure of the light which is pure and holy, may be guided; and so in the light walking and abiding, these may be fulfilled in the Spirit, not from the letter, for the letter killeth, but the Spirit giveth life.

You can almost feel "the Quaker thing" behind those words!

Minimum of ritual, and no holy days or consecrated buildings

As you will already have gathered, Quakers practise the greatest possible simplicity in their method of worship. At the intellectual level, the reason for this can be seen in the words of William Penn, written in 1693:

> This world is a form; our bodies are forms; and no visible acts of devotion can be without forms. But yet the less form in religion the better, since God is a Spirit; for the more mental our worship, the more adequate to the nature of God; the more silent, the more suitable to the language of the Spirit.[19]

This attitude to ritual applies particularly to those specially significant ceremonies which the Christian churches call "sacraments" - where the outward ritual is felt in a very special way to be a reflection of a transforming inward experience in those who take part. The traditional definition of a sacrament is "an outward and visible sign of an inward and spiritual grace". The spatial metaphor of "inward" and "outward" also appears frequently in Quaker writings, the inward always being regarded as having pre-eminence.

Attempts to interpret the metaphor in intellectual terms are pointless and unhelpful, because metaphors are not intended to operate at that level of discourse. If the Quaker thing really says something to you, you will have no difficulty in understanding what Friends have been feeling round for when they use this metaphor.

I must say something at this point in rough, non-scholarly terms, about the Quaker view of the sacraments, in case you belong to a church that has them. As you may know, at different times in Christian history there have been up to thirty sacraments practised, but in Britain the Anglican church recognises only two: baptism, and Eucharist or the Lord's Supper. The Roman Catholic church has five further ones: confirmation, penance, extreme unction (the ritual anointing of a dying person), orders (investing priests with spiritual authority) and matrimony.

With great theological precision, the Eucharist reminds the participants symbolically and with solemnity that the Creator so loved the world that he was prepared to enter His own creation, to be incarnate in a human being and submit patiently to being rejected and tortured to death by people who misused their free will to do so. The rite also impresses on them that God's grace is always there, objectively, simply waiting for them to accept it in obedience. The Eucharist is also a corporate act, signifying that God's incarnation unites believers to God and to one another.

The celebration of the sacraments, especially partaking in the Eucharist, is a vital part of the lives of many Christians. It renews their faith and helps them, often more than anything else can, to grapple with the changes and chances of this mortal life. Moreover, the celebration of special events in life seems to be a basic human need. A wedding, whether in a church or a registry office, is an occasion and people dress up for it; there would be a sense of outrage if a long-standing employee left his or her place of work without a presentation from colleagues; and at the national level there are occasions of rejoicing and mourning in which people feel involved. The services of the Christian churches, with their complex structures of praying, reading and singing, kneeling, sitting and standing, and the use of hallowed phrases of great antiquity, meet the same essential need. The non-conformist churches have broken away in varying degrees from these forms, but their services are still "occasions".

Why, then, have Friends gone to such lengths in dispensing with ritual? They would probably agree with most of those who practise rituals that no ceremony can be effective unless those participating really enter into the spirit of it. But "effective" and "really" are words that beg the question. How does the ceremony work on the participant? A well-conducted ceremony can create a wonderful atmosphere of worship; but there is the danger that it may be imagined to have an almost magical effect, regardless of any inward intention of the participant. This is apparent in relation to infant baptism, where the subject of the rite is clearly in no position to enter consciously into the proceedings.

Although Friends do not practise outward sacraments, it would not be true to say that they have no sacraments at all. They have always felt that if their religion was genuine their whole lives should be an outward and visible sign of it. They avoid labelling two aspects of their lives "sacred" and "secular". When the light of God shines in the heart, the inward-versus-outward problem disappears; the inward intention and the outward symbol - indeed, all outward acts of any kind - are seen as forming harmonious parts of their lives as a whole.

Consistently with this, they do not mark off Sunday or any other day as inherently more holy than other days; nor do they consecrate their meeting houses. They have found that they can worship God at any time and in any place where they gather together in the right spirit.

Obviously, this general approach to formal religion constitutes a bold objective. Some would say that it showed an egocentric spirit even to attempt to live like that - obeying only the spirit within. Nevertheless, Friends have found that strength is given if they sincerely ask for it; and however often they fall short of their aim they pick themselves up and go on again. And in the background there are always their times of communion with God and one another in their regular meetings for worship. It could not be claimed that these are not ceremonies at all: the circle or square of chairs, the table in the middle with flowers and books, the shaking of hands - all could be called ritualised. But the basic simplicity of the whole setup is an outward sign of the Quaker thing.

When the early Friends took the step of dropping outward physical ceremonies, it must have deeply shocked their devout neighbours, and added to the suspicion and hostility with which they were treated. The situation is now completely changed: there is much wider recognition in this century that people's spiritual needs vary enormously, and Friends' attitude to external ceremonies is now seldom seen as a criticism of the practices of others. It does not even prevent some Friends from taking part in the practices of churches that do have outward sacraments. I myself attend our local Anglican church and am courteously invited to take communion - which I do, on the occasions when I feel that the ceremony is "in the light" for me, as it usually is. Conversely, members of other churches are always welcome to worship with Friends. They are put under no pressure to change their allegiance, and both they and the meeting they visit gain from their presence. A senior Anglican clergyman has actually joined the Society of Friends without feeling any uneasiness about this dual membership.

No ordained ministers

Since Friends do not have special ceremonies, they naturally do not need specially appointed people to perform these; and not having dogmas means that there is no need for specially trained people to expound them. The priestly function goes deeper than that, however. An ordained priest is recognised by the members of his or her church as being vested with a certain spiritual authority, which is felt to have been handed down - often by the laying on of hands - in an unbroken line from the Christian apostles, that is, the disciples of Jesus plus one or two special missionaries like Paul of Tarsus.

Friends see this aspect of authority in a rather different light. For them, authority in matters of worship and ministry resides essentially in the worshipping group as a whole, here and now. The early Friends had a sense of the presence of the risen Jesus in their midst when they were gathered in their silent meetings for worship. There is indeed a famous painting showing a Quaker meeting with a diaphanous figure of Jesus hovering above it.

I should like to add here that their attitude towards the priestly function is not to be taken as reflecting adversely on the paid (though often rather poorly paid) clergy of the mainstream Christian churches. The position now is quite different from when the early Friends spoke scornfully of "hireling priests". At that time many of the clergy lived luxurious and worldly lives, and they were inevitably supporters of the political establishment. Most present-day clergy, to my knowledge, live arduous and dedicated lives, trying like the best of their predecessors down the centuries to carry out the command of Jesus to feed his sheep. It is saddening, however, that the validity or otherwise of the Orders of the different churches, and the continuing argument about the ordination of women, are still a ground of disunity in the Christian scene.

Is the Quaker thing Christian?

After what I have just written, you may well wonder whether the Quaker thing is so different from ordinary Christianity that it is a different religion altogether. Of course the answer depends on exactly what you mean by "Christian". For many centuries the meaning would have been quite clear: Christians were those who sincerely believed all the articles of the Nicene Creed. But nowadays people hold a wide range of belief (and lack of it), and many British people now belong to other faiths such as Islam, Hinduism, Rastafarianism and so on. Within Christianity, there is a great deal of diversity not only between the different denominations but within their membership. The same applies to the Society of Friends. Some Friends are willing, even eager, to call themselves Christian, while others are careful not to do so for fear of giving a false impression. This diversity is acknowledged, even welcomed.

Before I go any further, I would like to take you with me on a very amateurish tour of the Christian faith, looking at it as if we were outsiders encountering it for the first time. If you are already a practising Christian, try not to be offended at this rather bald description.

Whatever detractors may have said, often justly, about Christianity, and however much its practitioners may have let it down, it would be difficult to deny that the Judaeo-Christian world view summed up in the Nicene Creed is awe-inspiring both in its majesty and in its tenderness. It is not surprising that it has lasted 2,000 years and still commands some allegiance from a quarter of the population of the world. Against the vast backdrop of the universe, a personal yet more than personal God, having created that universe, created also human beings in some degree like himself: animals with self-consciousness and free will. A fantastically bold experiment, if nothing more. In the course of that experiment he appointed a special people, the Jews, to be bearers of his intention for the whole of humanity, hoping that in the end all people would use their free will to live according to his ordinance without any compulsion. When nevertheless they rebelled against him, after many interventions through specially gifted prophets he entered the stage himself - not with a flourish of trumpets, but as a human baby, who when grown to manhood would set out with great humility to show his creatures a better way. But in vain. When in their perversity they rejected him and put him to death by torture, he suffered this in a loving and forgiving spirit. Finally, by coming to life again he demonstrated that nothing in his universe can be lost, and that death is not an end but a beginning.

The portrait of the Creator as shown in Jesus became for many millions the great supporting and comforting symbol. He is the Good Shepherd who cares for his sheep and carries the lambs in his arms, and finally lays down his life for them. For the real believer he is still alive and caring for them. It is his voice that they hear in their hearts, his touch that heals the wound. His is the extra hand on the lone yachtsman's tiller. It is his presence that beckons them across the darkness from eternity. He is the final proof that we are not merely seeking but also being sought, that life is worth living, and that death itself shall not be conqueror. The Quaker poet John Greenleaf Whittier expressed this feeling in these stanzas from his poem *Our Master:*

No fable old, nor mythic lore,
Nor dream of bards and seers,
No dead fact stranded on the shore
Of the oblivious years;

But warm, sweet, tender, even yet
A present help is He;
And faith has still its Olivet,
And love its Galilee.

The healing of his seamless dress
Is by our beds of pain;
We touch him in life's throng and press
And we are whole again.

As I was writing this part of my letter, a well-known Friend, Walter Martin, who had given much service to the Society of Friends, was dying of motor neurone disease, an incurable condition in which the sufferer becomes completely paralysed over a number of years, and in the end is usually unable even to speak. With the last remaining vestige of movement in his hand, and using a special machine, he wrote an article in *The Friend* in which he summed up his spiritual state by quoting the concluding verses of Chapter 8 of Paul's letter to the Roman Christians:

For I am convinced that there is nothing in death or life, in the realm of spirits or superhuman powers, in the world as it is or the world as it shall be, in the forces of the universe, in heights or depths - nothing in all creation that can separate us from the love of God in Christ Jesus our Lord.

For our Friend, this great affirmation carried the same conviction as it has done to many others before him down the centuries, and - almost unbelievably - enabled him to count his blessings.

It would be unhelpful to start counting the plus and minus points for Christianity or any other religion. But it is an undoubted fact that the Christian faith has endowed many individuals with the will to do great works of mercy and the strength to carry them out. Many individual Christians are to be found helping others. They are prominent in most charities at home and overseas. They exert a strong influence among those who work for peace and the preservation of the environment. They are thick on the ground in such places as hospices for the dying and shelters for down-and-outs. It must be added at once, though, that atheists and humanists and members of every religion can be found doing similar works with equal commitment.

At the same time, the negative aspects of Christianity cannot and should not be ignored. The organised religion built on the Gospel record and tradition has often proved a monument to human frailty. According to the Gospel record itself, the followers of Jesus were quarrelling among themselves even when he was alive.[20] Within a few generations they were beginning to expel one another from the fellowship for holding different views as to his nature. It was common form for the various heretical propositions defined by councils of Christians to end by saying that anyone who believed them "let him be anathema" - that is, "accursed". Christians were so anxious to deify and define their founder that in large measure they lost sight of his teaching and example. In the end they began to imitate his enemies by putting one another to death for "heresy".

Moreover, the present century has seen the destruction and threatened destruction of whole sections of humanity, and the devastation of the earth, because people who call themselves Christian have been filled with fear and hatred of others. Other religions too have caused hatred and suffering for those who choose not to espouse them. Not surprisingly, many people now question whether religion has any value at all.

Personal difficulties in accepting the Christian faith are no less serious a matter than the more historical and political ones. At the intellectual level, the uncertainties I have mentioned about its origins, and the authenticity of Bible texts, are to many people an insuperable obstacle. Then there is the question of the exclusive claims of Christianity, and the position of the billions of people who will never hear of the Gospel. If Christians believed that God created these people, too, and would provide them with their own equally valid means of finding their way and obeying his commands, there would be no problem. But this is not the case: the claim that Christianity is the one and only true religion is built into the intellectual fabric of the faith. In fact, it is an inescapable conclusion if it is believed that God incarnated himself once and once only in human form. Few Christians still subscribe to the view - common as recently as 50 years ago - that there is some kind of inferior dispensation for people of other religions, provided they lead good lives (good by Christian standards), but that if a missionary preaches the Gospel to them and they reject it, as most of them do, they are condemned to unceasing torture in a life after death. Nevertheless, the "scandal of particularity" remains officially part of Christian doctrine, despite cautious attempts by some theologians to get away from it.[21]

The future of Christianity, at any rate in its simple credal form, is now in question - notwithstanding that a quarter of the world is still nominally Christian and that the Christian churches still have substantial political and social influence in many places. It is, I think, not too strong to say that Christianity, in Britain at any rate, is in a deep crisis of credibility.

Authority: in the end, personal responsibility and experience

The weakening of the influence of Christianity does not mean that the problem of authority with which I began this section will go away. On the contrary, it now presses on everyone with ever-increasing force. One thing is clear: a source of authority can't be found just by wishing for it, nor in the long run can beliefs be imparted by emotional pressure. As the early Quaker William Penn said, "Faith is a gift of God." It is true that some people have been converted either by evangelising campaigns or after agonising internal struggles, and that this has proved to be the right way for them; but many others (including myself) have found, often with equal pain and distress, that they were meant to travel by another path.

But by what other path? Do Quakers also claim that only their path is right? What I have written so far will, I think, make it clear that they do not make any such claim. There is no ultimate guarantee that what is seen by looking within is valid; the journey inwards may after all be the pursuit of a mirage. The Quaker way is just as self-validating as any other source of authority - indeed it is more frankly and openly so. There is no escape from the personal responsibility of deciding whether to follow it or not. Quakers can only say that they have discovered in experience that the attitude implicit in what I have been exploring with you is true and right *for them*. This has been the experience of Quakers from the earliest days of the movement. Here is Isaac Penington writing in 1662:

> When the principle of life is known, and that which God hath begotten felt in the heart, the distinction between what God opens and requires there, and what springs up in man's wisdom, reason and imagination, is very manifest.[22]

You can only find out for yourself whether Penington was right or not.

Quakers therefore cannot claim that their way is necessarily better than other ways, still less that it is the only true way. What keeps many of us on that path is this: that as we go along, we encounter special moments, in our silent meetings or at other times - a light not seen but sensed, a voice not speaking but heard, touches not felt but known. Again and again we are convinced that we are on one of the highways of the great Spirit, that it is a privilege to walk there, and that we must walk on, however often we may stumble or fall.

With that I come to the kernel of what I have been struggling to say for many pages. Perhaps you will now understand why I said at the start that the Quaker thing can't really be reduced to words? - particularly to modern words. It is a strange and rather exasperating fact that the most apt and expressive words about the Quaker thing are still those used by the first Friends. With their 17th century English they seemed to have a genius for finding the telling phrase, and it is still very difficult to find equally effective expressions in modern English.

Among their favourite images were the Light, the Seed, the Life, Christ the Inward Teacher, and "that of God in everyone". Changes in language and culture have taken away from us something of the freshness, precision and force of these old phrases; but they still point towards different aspects of the basic experience. The Light of God illuminates the heart and the conscience. The Seed that is somehow God grows in us; the Life springs from gathering with others in the presence of God. Christ the Inward Teacher hints at something far more important and fundamental than the Christ of history. And finally, "that of God in everyone" expresses the conviction that the Creator so loves all created things as to give something of divinity to them to lighten their darkness and show them the way if they will but look inward and find it.

The phrase "that of God in everyone" is perhaps the nearest thing there is to a Quaker dogma. It carries with it the danger attaching to all dogmas: when too easily used, it can become a cliché and lead to misunderstanding. Friends themselves have sometimes made the mistake of using this phrase to mean simply "a good streak" in what is otherwise bad or indifferent in someone. In a sense it does mean that, but it has far wider implications, as I think you will realise. Sometimes "that of God" is conceived as a kind of separate organ or a little spark; but that is still rather misleading. In fact the phrase does not denote an object at all. It is not even a mood or a state of mind. It refers to a relationship, a process of knowing that goes on in each person, whether from our point of view they seem to be good or bad, and whether we like them or not. It is also the potential for seeing ourselves as we really are. For me, one of the best hints at it in modern English is in a poem written by Martha Whitehead, a Friend, when she was thirteen years old:

> There's something inside me.
> It doesn't want to get out -
> It's a part of me
> But it's different.
> It's very aware.
> It can help and guide
> And I can trust it.
> It is in me
> But it is in everyone.
> In each it is separate
> Continuous
> Caring in everything
> Caring for everything.
> It waits for anything and everything.
> It is always present.

Attempts at expressing the Quaker thing directly in words will always fail, but that doesn't mean that it isn't real. The "openings" may come and go, but the underlying experience is always there, and Quakers have learnt to base their whole lives upon it.

IV

The Quaker Thing
in Daily Life
and Personal
Relationships

All aspects of life affected

THE QUAKER THING DOES not only operate on Sundays. Friends do indeed bring their joys and sorrows, their successes and failures, into their silent meetings; but what they experience there deeply affects the way they live. There is a two-way traffic between the inward and the outward aspects of their lives. The sacred and the secular are not kept in watertight compartments.

As a result, Quakers tend to develop a characteristic pattern of attitudes and practices in their life-styles, relationships at work, social and political activities, recreations - everything. You don't find the whole package in every Friend, and individual items can be seen in people of all religions and none. But if you notice most of it you are probably in the presence of an actual or potential Quaker.

These attitudes and practices are not worked out by an intellectual system, nor are they embodied in fixed regulations. They are more a distinctive stance, a way. They are broadly indicated in the *Advices and Queries* I referred to earlier. I will now go over a few of them in some detail and give you some references so that you can explore in greater depth any that may specially interest you.

Peace and harmlessness

If there is one Quaker attitude which underlies all the others, it is peacefulness and harmlessness towards other human beings and the whole of creation. Logically, the position is clear: if all people have "that of God" in them, then deliberately trying to injure or kill them, whether in war or in any other context, is an offence not merely against humanity but against God - whatever you conceive to lie behind that word. But real peacefulness goes beyond logic. It implies a certain attitude of one's whole being. In practical terms it means trying to work harmoniously with other people, even when they are hostile; avoiding talking in a hurtful or negative way on any subject, or allowing one's feelings - even warm and generous feelings - to betray one into saying anything that is unfair or untrue. In short, it means always asking oneself: "How is what I am doing or saying going to feel at the receiving end?"

Living like this undoubtedly calls for discipline, and that can only be attained by cultivating an inner coolness and recollectedness among the many often harassing activities of daily life. A good way of reaching that state is to set aside at least a short period of each day for inward retirement; but if the pressures of life prevent you from keeping this up, there is no cause to feel guilty or despairing. If you are really trying to follow the Quaker way, the sudden inward flash will come, when that which is within us but also outside us illuminates the troubled scene and brings guidance and confidence.

For some people this illumination takes the form of a joyful moment of communion with God, whose presence is felt as a loving parent. For others it is a sense of the comradeship of a Jesus who is alive though unseen to the outward eye. To many of us nowadays the experience comes rather as a spirit, a presence, which assumes no human form, but is a no less real or trustworthy guide. Friends, while being strongly aware of their imperfections, do not feel separated from God. They see themselves rather as integral parts of a grand mysterious whole that is somehow ultimately "right" - even if it were to destroy them. They experience something within them, nearer than hands or feet or breathing, which shows up their dark sides, but at the same time points the way out of their perplexities. Yet that something is outside them as well; they do not draw a line between *in here* and *out there.* In their very seeking they are being sought; they know and feel that they are also known. Moreover, they feel that although that which created personality must in some sense be personal, there is something behind it which is beyond all names and forms but yet is to be trusted; that somewhere in the recesses of the human psyche the same spirit must be at work in those of different faiths and none, whatever the feelings, or opinions, or concepts in which it finds expression.

In this experience of unity, in whatever form it presents itself, is rooted the power to practise harmlessness in life and to bring peace and reconciliation into our little corner of the world. It is there in the depths of every human being, waiting to be released. For Quakers it is of particular significance, because it underlies their conscientious objection to all war, and to the recognition of their Society as one of the traditional "peace churches".

Religious toleration

For religious people, being peaceful means nothing if it doesn't include being peaceful among themselves. Forming as they do a visible part of the Christian scene, this is a fundamental and in some ways embarrassing issue for Quakers. It is a puzzling and sombre fact that Christians, who follow one who taught and practised love and harmlessness towards others, should have the worst record of any world religion for intolerance and persecution, not merely of members of other religions but of one another. There has been some improvement in recent years, but bitter controversy continues and Quakers themselves are not wholly exempt from it.

It is an essential fruit of the Quaker thing, wherever it takes root and grows in people's hearts, to tolerate the religious views of other people. And toleration in this context doesn't mean just cynically shrugging off views you think are unsound or harmful. Nor, on the other hand, does it mean looking pityingly at those who hold different views and trying by every available means of persuasion to convert them to the truth - i.e. your view. Toleration, if it is to be worth anything, must at least mean realising that, however confident you may feel in the truth of your own view, we all "see in a mirror indistinctly"[23] and may therefore be partly mistaken in what we think we see.

But true toleration is at a much higher level than that. It means accepting in your very heart that, notwithstanding differences in outward form and expression, other people may have insights as valid for them as yours are for you. That state is not to be reached by any intellectual process, nor is there much emotion in it, nor can it be attained by any effort of will or psychological technique. The word "compromise" does not apply to it, for it is absolute. It needs no response from others, for it extends to those who deny its validity or regard it as sinful. It can only be hinted at in words. Here is what an early Friend, Isaac Penington, wrote in the midst of the persecution of Quakers in the 17th century:

> This is the true ground of love and unity, not that such a man walks and does just as I do, but because I feel the same spirit and life in him, and that he walks in his rank, in his own order, in his proper way and place of subjection to that; and this is far more pleasing to me than if he walked just in that track wherein I walk. Nay so far as I am spiritual, I cannot so much as desire that he should do so, until he be particularly led thereto by the same Spirit which led me.... [24]

Isaac Penington was writing of toleration between Christians. But, surprisingly in such an intolerant age, the 17th century Quakers showed tolerance towards other religions. William Penn wrote:

> The humble, meek, merciful, just, pious, and devout souls are everywhere of one religion; and when death has taken off the mask they will know one another, though the divers liveries they wear here makes them strangers.[25]

In the 18th century, the American Quaker John Woolman was even more explicit:

> There is a principle which is pure, placed in the human mind, which in different places and ages hath had different names; it is, however, pure and proceeds from God. It is deep, and inward, confined to no forms of religion, nor excluded from any, where the heart stands in perfect sincerity. In whomsoever this takes root and grows, of what nation soever, they become brethren in the best sense of the expression.[26]

Having said that, however, I have to admit that although the great majority of Friends behave in a fully tolerant manner, this is not always the case. Friends are human beings and not saints. Controversies about Quaker faith and practice have been common in the Society from the beginning, and if you attend Quaker meetings for a time you will become aware of controversy, some of it in less than tolerant vein. It may give you a further insight into the Quaker thing if I muse a little on the differences.

Current differences arise over several issues: between Friends who are anxious to be visibly identified as "Christian" and see themselves as entrusted with promulgating a special Christian message taught by George Fox, and those who are cautious about adopting a Christian or any other label; between those who feel that sexual relationships other than within monogamous marriage are wrong, and those who feel or experience them as valid ways of expressing love; and between those who feel they must urgently campaign for peace or a more responsible attitude to the environment, and those who see the nurture of inward stillness as their prime concern. Many Friends do not see these questions in terms of "either-or", and where arguments arise they mainly come from a vocal minority, with the rest of Friends exercising gentle restraint. But the views of a minority are never ignored, because they may turn out to be prophetic rather than mistaken. They are always tested against the leadings of the group as a whole. [27]

I hope you will not be put off because you occasionally hear dogmatic or intolerant voices in the meetings you attend. As you gradually come to experience that which binds Friends together, the differences among them will seem less important. You will quite likely find that Friends who seem to be at the extreme ends of the spectrum of religious experience are among the most loved and trusted members of their Meetings.

Simplicity of life-style

Another sign of the presence of the Quaker thing in a person is a tendency to live in a simple, uncluttered style. This passage from the journal of the American Friend John Woolman (1720-1772) may give you some feeling for the prompting behind this tendency:

My mind through the power of Truth was in good degree weaned from the desire of outward greatness, and I was learning to be content with real conveniences that were not costly; so that a way of life free from Entanglements, appeared best for me, tho' the income was small. I had several offers of business that appeared profitable, but saw not my way clear to accept of them, as believing that the business proposed would be attended with more outward care and cumber than was required of me to engage in. I saw that a humble man, with the Blessing of the Lord, might live on a little, and that where the heart was set on greatness, success in business did not satisfie the craving; but that commonly with an increase of wealth, the desire for wealth increased. There was a care on my mind so to pass my time, as to things outward, that nothing might hinder me from the most steady attention to the voice of the True Shepherd. [28]

For some Quakers nowadays simplicity of lifestyle is not a problem, since contrary to popular belief there are quite poor Quakers, though a few are rich. The moderately well-off majority tend to experience a certain interior tension which they find difficult to resolve. On the one hand they are conscious not merely of those starving in other countries but also of the many living near or below the margin of subsistence here in Britain. In this country we have a social framework which is politically and socially determined mainly by people seeking physical comfort, labour-saving devices, electronic amusements, foreign holidays, and getting ahead in their careers. Friends are well aware that these are mere dreams for many people. On the other hand, they have the same natural desire as anyone else to provide a decent living for themselves and their families. So what does a middle-income Quaker family do about a car to carry the babies and their gear, a washing machine for their grubby clothes, a school where they will be well-taught, books to encourage them to read widely, concerts and electronic equipment to introduce them to music, theatre visits to stimulate their imagination, exhibitions to sensitise them to art, and foreign travel to show them how other people live?

Early Friends took the ideal of simplicity very seriously, at any rate so far as their places of worship and their dress were concerned. They adopted a radical attitude towards dress that in hindsight is difficult not to regard as mistaken. Around 1700, soon after the persecution had ceased, they began to adopt the characteristic "uniform" shown on the Quaker Oats packet, and unfortunately they rather pressurised one another into this, despite protests from wiser members, including George Fox's widow Margaret. She wrote: "We must look at no colours nor make anything that is changeable colours as the hills are, nor sell them nor wear them, but we must be all in one dress and one colour: this is a silly poor Gospel." [29]

But the simple dress prevailed, and a few went on wearing it until quite recent times. Friends on this occasion failed to realise that to signify an inward and spiritual thing by a conspicuous outward sign could finish up by denying the thing itself; in this case, by concentrating so much on how many buttons and what constituted a frill that they spent more energy on what they wore, rather than less.

I hope this cautionary tale will disabuse you of any idea that Friends always reach the ideals they aim at.

Perhaps early Friends should not be too severely criticised. Trying to work out a life-style for a Quaker in the present-day world leads to a mass of dilemmas and contradictions. And there is a real problem. There is enough food, raw materials and renewable sources of energy for everyone to have a decent standard of living, provided the world's population does not increase much beyond what it is now. So the blame for poverty must rest on people. But on whom? It could be argued that poverty exists because some people have worked the system to secure more than average incomes, and pay a police force to defend their positions. It could further be argued that these people's demands distort the economies of their countries into producing non-essential goods at the expense of essential food and shelter. On the other hand, one could point to people who have made large fortunes without apparently behaving dishonestly or injuring others - indeed, rich entrepreneurs could be claimed to provide work for many people through their initiative. By the same reasoning it could be suggested that by living austerely one is putting people out of work. Against that, it could be argued that the whole system by which the livelihood of the many is at the mercy of the relatively few is inherently immoral. The economic and political framework of life imposes itself on everybody, privileged and disadvantaged alike, and attempts at doing anything helpful often seem pointless or even self-defeating.

Is there a Quaker talisman to help the individual to find a way through this maze of conflicting arguments? There is not, but there does seem to be a tie-up between the Quaker thing and the uneasiness that produces the arguments. Both the yearning for simplicity of life and the deep uneasiness about the misery in the world refuse to go away. What can a Friend do?

Some Friends respond by looking carefully at their spending. They see no harm done if they earn up to or even more than the national average, if it can be done honestly and on merit. But when it comes to buying a particular item of goods or services they tend to ask themselves: (1) Will it make me wiser, and better able to play my full part in the world? (2) Is it beautiful (as opposed to scarce or fashionable)? (3) Does it give me innocent enjoyment? (4) Shall I be using it at least in part to bring help or enjoyment to others? (5) Am I sure that the manufacture of it does not involve injury to others, e.g. through industrial disease or poor employment practices? (6) Am I sure that it does not harm the natural environment? (7) Most important of all, shall I be upset if I lose it?

If a middle-income family lives like that, it can usually afford to contribute to charitable work that helps disadvantaged people at home and abroad. This is not an ideal solution, but it does at least help - especially when it is accompanied by keeping in touch with the work that is being done, and if possible lending a hand oneself.

I think it is not a valid objection that helping in this way prevents reform of the system. It seems sufficient to mention that before the war I was being urged by well-meaning people not to support the voluntary hospitals because that would prevent the introduction of a national health service! Nor is it a valid counter-argument that the National Health Service only came about as a result of the war. The historical process doesn't work like that. It is full of accidents and surprises. Causes can never be fully analysed or effects fully foreseen.

Some Friends, however, feel that this whole approach is too much of a compromise. Living in the midst of an exploitative society, they feel that they are in danger of denying their own principles by the way they live. Some who feel like that have tried to establish a higher moral standard by setting up communities. This movement focused informally in the Towards Community group, which was formed in 1974. Communities of this kind are not confined to isolated rural areas; there is in fact one in the East End of London. Nor do they have to live in a single building. What is essential is that the members live in a way that does not injure others or the environment, and that they share resources.

Living with others is not however an easy matter. Many intentional communities have failed due to internal disputes about objectives or differences of temperament, and some have become inward-looking and failed to care for the wider community around them. The whole question of setting up such communities was explored in a symposium of thoughtful essays entitled *Towards Community*, published by the group.

Finally, the William Allen Society, a body founded by a few Friends and named after an early Victorian Quaker chemist, scientist and philanthropist, has refurbished old houses in London in which people of different family circumstances can form units that provide mutual help and support.[30] This is the great virtue of communities, as well as the ability to live in a fairly simple style.

In the end, I have to leave it to you to explore for yourself how the Quaker thing, if you find it working within you, will influence your life-style. Like so much else in the Quaker way, there is no ideal, no blueprint; only imperfect people trying to be obedient to "the promptings of love and truth in their hearts".

Integrity in business and financial affairs

Strict integrity in business and financial dealings, carried sometimes to the point of avoiding all speculation, has always been a part of the Quaker way. This has had considerable influence on the development of the Society of Friends. In 17th century England people had to bargain with shopkeepers over every purchase. Quaker shopkeepers, however, settled on a fair price and refused to depart from it. At first they lost custom and were laughed at, but very soon their method paid off. People found that they could rely on Quakers to treat them fairly; they could even send a child to buy something without fear of being cheated. When as a result Quakers prospered, they were envied by other traders - which may well have contributed to their being persecuted.

Friends also feel anything in the nature of gambling to be wrong. Most of them therefore do not take part in lotteries or hold premium bonds; but as always there is no rigid rule. Friends are expected to decide for themselves, on the basis of conscience, whether they should or should not take part in what many people regard as harmless activities.

As with other Quaker practices, you can't actually trace a connection between the Quaker thing and these attitudes to trade and moneymaking. Of course there are fairly obvious ethical arguments: speculative practices easily lead to unfair treatment of individuals; in any case they imply getting something for nothing at the expense of other people. Gambling also leads to preoccupation with possessions, and with some people it can become a destructive addiction. But these are only attempts to explain something that lies beyond the reach of explanation.

No swearing of legal oaths

Friends have always refused to swear legal oaths, because doing so implies that there are two standards of truthfulness and that you can only tell the truth with the support of some supernatural power - and with the threat of retribution in the background. Friends can also cite some words of Jesus of Nazareth in support of their position.[31]

In the early days of the Quaker movement, this peculiarity not only reinforced the prejudice against them but gave the authorities a pretext for persecuting them. This was done by requiring Friends to take the oath of allegiance to the King, and when they refused imprisoning them, as was lawfully possible at the time. With the Toleration Act of 1689 it became permissible for Friends to "affirm" instead of swearing on the Bible. This compromise removed the superstitious element of an oath, but has not fully overcome the objection that oath-taking under any guise implies a double standard of truth. Affirmation was not accepted by universities or Parliament until into the 19th century, so that for nearly two centuries Friends were debarred from those institutions.

Equal treatment of all people

An obvious implication of recognising "that of God" in everyone is that a Quaker should try to treat everyone alike: not kow-towing to people who happen to be more socially or intellectually important, or expecting deference from those who are poor or uneducated. The early Friends insisted on addressing everybody, regardless of worldly rank, with the familiar "thou" or "thee", instead of the deferential "you", and they refused to doff their hats or bow or scrape to anyone. When arraigned before the justices for their dissenting beliefs and practices, they refused to take off their hats in court. These peculiarities got them into further trouble, and many of them were imprisoned for contempt.

Nowadays hardly any Quakers use "thee" and "thou" or refuse to use courtesy titles. But the underlying point remains and is as relevant as ever, and putting it into effect is still neither inwardly nor outwardly easy. Among other things it means trying to subdue one's own class and race prejudices and then approaching in a loving spirit people who show such prejudices - even though this may entail refusing to consent, even by silence, to racist talk. An example of how difficult it is to root out such prejudices is related by a white Friend teacher, who had been discussing with colleagues, on the basis of written reports, what provision should be made for a specially gifted child. She then had to admit to a sense of shock when the child proved to be black - and an even greater shock to find herself shocked. The unfounded assumption that black people are inherently less gifted had penetrated her subconscious more than she realised.

Quakers have from the beginning aimed at a high degree of sexual equality, and spoken ministry in meetings for worship has always been open equally to men and women. Although there was, and still is, less sexism in the Society of Friends than in society at large, Friends can't claim to have a completely clean sheet. For many years men and women met separately in business meetings, and the men's meetings usually had the greater influence in the Society's affairs. It was not until 1898 that the Society's top governing body, the Yearly Meeting, became equally open to women and men.

There is now almost complete equality in all the offices in the Society, but the sexist element in society generally, though weaker nowadays, still exerts some influence. In reaction to the sexism problem, an informal Quaker Women's Group was formed, and in 1986 a Swarthmore Lecture[32] given by some of its members jolted other Friends into recognising that there is still a long way to go before this form of discrimination is removed.

In taking the surprisingly egalitarian attitude that he did in the 17th century, George Fox cited Paul's words in Galatians 3.28 that "there is neither Jew nor Greek, there is neither bond nor free, there is neither male nor female: for ye are all one in Christ Jesus"; but the principle lies deeper than the expression of it in Christian or any other terms. The real issue is not about men and women, but about the feminine and masculine tendencies which form essential elements in everyone's make-up. These tendencies are not confined to one sex or the other, but are present in varying proportions in both men and women. The ideal is not a struggle, or even a dialogue, between the two tendencies, but a balance. Most Friends intuitively espouse that ideal, though without being able or willing to say why.

Sexual relationships

Friends are popularly supposed to be puritanical about sex and everything else, but if you explore at all deeply you will find that the influence of the Quaker thing on all personal conduct is much more subtle than that. Sex and marriage matter tremendously in everyone's life, including mine and no doubt yours. So it may give you some insight into the general climate of mind and spirit that Friends bring to moral questions if I now try to say something about Quaker views on sex.

This is an almost impossible subject to write about. It arouses passions and prejudices and is shot through with contradictions and paradoxes. The real snag is that what is actually *done* in sexual relations is at a different level from anything that can be *said*. Making love and talking about sex are on parallel lines that never meet. We have to face the fact that our private lives, and the very existence of humankind, rest on an instinctive function which would often be regarded as obscene if described in detail, but which is felt by those performing it to be a sacred and precious gift. I once heard a prosaic humanist psychotherapist say in a tone of awe and reverence: "I see the bed of the lovers stretching out to embrace the stars."

And reverence is not out of place. In that bed, time dissolves into eternity, the past and the future are reconciled, all the contrary things in the world become one. And through that reconciliation streams the whole flow of human life. Inadequate and unrealistic as writings about romantic love are, they reflect a universal feeling that deep in the sweaty earthiness there is a clear eternal diamond - something for which only the word "holy" is good enough.

The jewel, however, is inseparable from its setting, which can be of base metal. Against the ideal of romantic love has to be set a whole library of tension, jealousy, boredom and sorrow. Even children can be a burden and a disappointment as well as a joy and a triumph. You may say, "We know that". Intellectually, perhaps we do, but accepting the facts of our sexual lives with our whole being is nothing like so easy. Moreover, this is not necessarily the fault of the lovers.

Society does not discreetly leave them to the privacy of their own bed, but regulates their relationship by laws and customs which they break at their peril. Up to a point this may amount to a healthy discipline; but there seems nearly always to be a measure of conflict between the lovers and their surroundings.

This is not altogether surprising when one considers two hard facts. First, there is an enormous variation from one person to another in the force and nature of their sexual drive, as well as their ways of expressing it. It can vary from almost total lack of interest to an insatiable craving. It can be associated with a wide variety of images of what the desired one is like and is there for. And the sexual feelings of quite a proportion of people are for their own sex - and, for other people, that is so for a proportion of the time.

Secondly, there seems to be no universal overriding norm of sexual behaviour. "Almost without exception, human societies all over the world have evolved complex codes of behaviour, the breaking of which is in some regarded with tolerance, in others punished with death.... Love-play between children, paederasty, adult homosexuality, free heterosexual relations between the young unmarried or between the married, each of these can, in different societies, be rigidly forbidden, tolerated, or encouraged." This quotation is from a book entitled *Towards a Quaker View of Sex* [33] produced in the early 1960s by a group of professionally well qualified Quakers. They had been faced with the confusion and uncertainty of young people growing up in a social scene where their difficulties had been compounded by the rapidly changing mores of the present century. The writers noted that the position of traditional Christianity in this situation had become painful and difficult. The mainstream churches had for centuries supported popular feeling in enforcing a rigid conventional pattern of conduct which could, and often did, operate with great cruelty on those who could not or would not conform to it. Claims to high moral values were often accompanied by an insensitivity to the real needs of human beings which left some people untouched and others desperate. Intellectually, this sort of conduct was underpinned by perverting the Jewish myth of Adam and Eve (which is about the growth of humankind towards free-will and adult responsibility) to mean that sexual relations were to be equated with "original sin".

The authors of the book were led to look deeply at the whole question of sexual values. Monogamous marriage did seem to be an ideal in British society, they concluded, and wayward sexuality could be appallingly destructive. But many patterns were possible and in fact existed. There was no escaping the fact that a conventional marriage could be a source of disharmony and bitterness, while an unconventional relationship, judged by any tests you like to apply - emotional harmony, truly loving behaviour, good health, good adjustment of children, caring for those outside the relationship, depth of spiritual life of those concerned - could be "in right ordering".

In looking for sounder moral guidelines the authors agreed that sexual activity has to be disciplined, and that this is not purely a private matter. Measures are needed to preserve family life, protect children, and above all to prevent the exploitation of one person by another. But worldly laws and customs that ignore the grace of God will never be enough. The ideal is therefore a positive morality based on an internal spiritual discipline. This is actually more severe than an external moral code. Nevertheless, if we genuinely want to do God's will, strength is given, including the strength to say No to ourselves and others when the occasion demands it.

These, broadly speaking, are the views of the authors of the book. Some of their views, for instance on incest and child abuse, are now known to be inadequate, but the rest were astonishingly farsighted, and many - perhaps most - Friends probably think more or less likewise.

But not all. When the book was first published in 1963, a deep difference of opinion appeared in the Society. An influential group of Friends ultimately persuaded the Society's national executive committee, Meeting for Sufferings*, almost to disown the book. There were resignations on both sides of the issue. Since then horizons

---

* *So-called because early Friends' affairs needed to be dealt with by a meeting for business while they were suffering in jail.*

have probably widened - but AIDS and politicians' strictures about non-adherence to "family values" have intervened. (The process leading to the publication of *Quaker Faith & Practice* in 1994 showed that these issues can still rend the hearts of Friends. - EDITOR)

In practice, there are many Friends who take an understanding, even unshockable, attitude towards the sexual lives of themselves and other people. The real issue is: how does the Quaker thing influence the actual conduct of Friends in this regard? Surely it ought to be helpful? Shouldn't it lead to a view of something larger than simply *relationship*: a feeling of unity, not merely with one another but with the whole scheme of things? - a sense of the perennial grace of God in every situation - a grace beyond what either party could have received separately? Does it work out that way?

It should. But Friends are not superhuman. They are subject to the same failings as everyone else: the same temptation to invest emotionally in the one area where the individual really seems to count, the same tendency to start out with an ideal image of the partner which does not entirely correspond to reality. One can so easily ascribe to the other virtues of patience and faithfulness that he or she does not possess, and fail to appreciate the warmth and idealism that he or she does.

Moreover, without exception, the partners bring the dark sides of their characters into the partnership. So it will always contain the pairs of emotional opposites: the pleasures and the pains, the achievements and the vexations, the excitement and the boredom, the affectionate touch and the sudden inexplicable angry reaction. Some of these gradually become family jokes, but there will be deeper wounds that bring the little drama of the family home near to tragedy. Sometimes things build up to a crisis, after which the lovers may be able to make a fresh start on a more realistic footing, seeing each other more nearly as they are and accepting that what the other really thinks is unknowable. When that situation is reached, the partner can be cared for, yet not clutched to oneself as a means to one's own happiness. Even if at first this all seems a second best, it can in the long run turn out to be the best of all. A new kind of love - cool, peaceful, even impartial, but reliable and infinitely precious - seems to invade the house from nowhere.

But the mystery will always remain. Another psychotherapist once said to me, again in awed tones: "We don't know what makes a marriage work...."

Divorce

For many people the ideal of a long-lasting marriage is not realised. We live in a country and a time when sexual relations and family life are in a puzzling and disappointing state. There has been a steady trend towards greater freedom in relations between the sexes, a reduction in sexual discrimination, the development of counselling, and the emergence of more mentally healthy and non-judgmental attitudes. But these do not seem to have led to any improvement in marital happiness or stability - rather the reverse. More than one in three marriages now end in irretrievable breakdown.

This prompts the question as to what Quakers feel about divorce, their own or other people's. Do Friends allow the remarriage of divorced people? About divorce one thing at least is certain: it is a shattering personal tragedy to those concerned. A Friend once described the effect on her as "a kind of bereavement". There is something deeply spiritual about full sexual union and a life in partnership, even when it fails to work out in daily life. It is not surprising that those who enter on a second marriage only do so after very careful thought, and often with a sense of guilt and anxiety.

When a divorced person wishes to marry again according to Friends' ways, consent is nearly always given. The great majority of Friends feel that, so far from refusing to bless a second attempt, they would see it as their duty to reassure the partners in the new marriage and try to heal the wounds created by the past.

Sex outside marriage

Sexual relationships between unmarried people are now common in society at large and are not nearly so heavily disapproved of as they were in previous generations. Many young couples now live together instead of, or before, getting married. Many people are inclined to say that there is nothing inherently immoral in this. Clearly, having children without setting up a stable home is less than fair to them, but modern methods of contraception can deal with this problem.

What then is the Quaker moral attitude? There is such a deep mystery - and terror - about sexual relationships, and almost everyone wonders about the implications. Sooner or later, what begins with an instinctual reaction grows into a complex relationship, and questions arise about its future. Any attempt to regulate this highly diverse and individual process would be a hopelessly blunt instrument, and ordinary secular society seems at last to have recognised this. Where the Quaker thing is relevant is that it leads Friends to emphasise the deep seriousness and responsibility of close relationships, and equally to avoid laying down rigid formulated rules.

On extramarital relations on the part of people already married, the moral position might seem to be more clear-cut. The integrity of the family is paramount, and in secular British society the nuclear family is the norm. The issue is not, however, simply that extramarital sexual relationships can lead to jealousy and negative emotions that damage the atmosphere of the home. What begins as a natural mutual urge soon develops psychological and spiritual depths, even when there may be no actual physical intercourse, which is difficult for anyone to experience with more than one person at a time - though there are exceptions. Without going outside my own circle I know of more than one marriage which seems actually to have benefited from the extramarital relationship of one of the partners.

For many of those who are trying to follow the Quaker way, it is no longer possible to rely simply on either one's emotions or on the conventions of secular society. "That of God" in oneself has to be brought into consultation as an inward coolness that decides, directs and governs our actions. The discipline that this leads to is in practice more, not less, demanding than any worldly convention or outward religious sanction.

Homosexuality

There is a one in three chance that you have had homosexual experience at some time in your life, and a one in ten chance that you are still attracted to people of your own sex. (Even these figures may be unreliable.) These are facts of human life, regardless of nation, class, race, profession, religion or any other outward circumstance. In Victorian times the British developed a phobia about this which has still not entirely disappeared. Until 1967 homosexual acts between males were illegal, and people were imprisoned for them. Publication of *Towards a Quaker View of Sex* was prompted in part by the misery created by this situation, and contributed in small part to changing the law. There is still legal discrimination against homosexuals in relation to the age of consent, and certainly there is prejudice against homosexuals in society generally.

In 1973, David Blamires wrote *Homosexuality from the Inside*, published by Quaker Home Service, and in 1982 a number of other Friends came out publicly in a pamphlet called *Meeting Gay Friends*. Since then, for all but those who grew up in fear of their state, it has been possible for gay people to be completely open among Friends. Some of the Society's most loved and trusted members are gay or lesbian. If you yourself are gay you are unlikely to encounter prejudice except from a very tiny minority (including some who are understandably agitated about the spread of AIDS). There is a Gay and Lesbian Fellowship and a Bisexual Group, both of which are informal and friendly. They continue, in recognition of the fact that it is still difficult not to be fully heterosexual in Britain today.

Food, drink and drugs

The Society of Friends has no dietary rules, but Quakers tend to have some recognisable habits. Long before nutrition became a common topic on the media, many Friends felt instinctively that what is now called a whole-food diet would be right for them. This means living on foods from which nothing has been taken away by refining, or preservatives added, and which, ideally, have been grown by organic methods without the use of artificial fertilisers or pesticides.

Many Friends also feel led to being vegetarian, and if you go to any Quaker gathering where food is served you will certainly find provision for this, if the whole menu is not vegetarian. One reason for becoming vegetarian is that it seems morally wrong to kill animals, or to rear them by the cruel and unnatural methods which are now common in large-scale and intensive farming. Another reason is that when so many people are undernourished, even starving, it seems wrong to convert vegetable products into meat and so lose more than half of their original food value.

Most Friends would probably find it difficult to explain their attitudes to these issues. They just have a general feeling that they ought to live in harmony with the living world, and that real health - physical, mental and spiritual - depends on their behaving in that spirit. As to how that harmony is to be attained, they respect one another's approaches. You will not be pressed to become a vegetarian or a vegan if you consort with Friends - though you might one day discover that you have developed a "stop in your mind" (to use an old Quaker phrase) against, for example, eating poultry grown in batteries. Personally I never eat veal now, because it cannot be produced without cruelty to the calves, and I am getting more and more uneasy about eating other kinds of meat.

Most Quakers also agree to differ about drinking alcohol. Many drink in moderation, and heavy drinkers and alcoholics are rare. Some are strictly teetotal, and a few of these campaign vigorously to persuade others to be so. All Friends, however, are aware of the dangers of the excessive use of alcohol, and they are quite clear that drinking and driving is altogether wrong, since it endangers the lives of other people. In deference to those who don't drink, alcohol is not permitted on Friends' premises - even at wedding receptions - and premises are not let to bodies concerned with the production or distribution of alcoholic drinks.

Alcohol is of course a drug, in the sense that it affects the human body and mind. The cups of tea and coffee that "cheer but not inebriate" are, strictly speaking, also drugs, mild as their effects are. Some Friends avoid them, and when coffee is served at Friends' functions, fruit juices, coffee substitutes and herb teas are sometimes available too. Some Friends are also aware that coffee and tea producers may be involved in unethical employment and sales practices.

When it comes to really potent drugs, Friends are instinctively wary. Even the drugs prescribed by the medical profession are distrusted for their side-effects, and you will find that quite a number of Friends prefer the gentler remedies prescribed by herbalists and homeopathic doctors.

As you might expect, Friends avoid the illegal use of drugs, not only because of their harmful effects, but because their views on integrity lead them to obey all just and reasonable laws of the state. They are aware of the anomalous position of cannabis, which seems on medical evidence to be less addictive and dangerous to health than tobacco, though some might describe it as the heart of a drug-based subculture. They have formed no view on whether it would help to decriminalise cannabis. On one legal but addictive drug which is now known to be very harmful, Friends are almost (but not quite) unanimous: tobacco. Smoking is not allowed on Meeting House premises, and it would be almost unthinkable in a Friends' meeting of any kind.

Seen from the Quaker angle, addiction in any form is a serious danger, not merely physically and mentally, but spiritually, even when it arises in entirely legal and seemingly harmless ways. Eating too much or unsuitable food, playing too hard at sport, sitting for hours in front of a computer or television, studying some pet subject into the small hours, or even working at one's daily job in an uncontrolled way, can be just as harmful as drinking alcohol or misusing drugs. All addictions in some degree weaken the command which "that of God" in an individual has over their life and hinders them from exercising the personal responsibility which is somehow implicit in the Quaker way.

How to live up to it ?

I wonder what you make of these "testimonies", to use the rather grand word by which Quakers often describe them? To many people they present a puzzling twofold paradox. The Quaker thing can't be spelt out in words; it has no thought-out theology or ethical code; even *Advices and Queries* are no more than hints and reminders. Yet, without much obvious logical connection, it results in definite attitudes and practices, some at least of which are disturbing to the general public and uncomfortable for Quakers themselves. Furthermore, these practices seem to be mainly negative - no participation in war, no luxurious living, no cheating or gambling, no discrimination by race or sex. Yet they seem to add up to a positive and active style of life.

There is no intellectual answer to these apparent contradictions. All one can say is that the Quaker thing is there, somewhere in the deep heart's core, giving a little nudge now and then. Sometimes "that of God", or whatever else you like to call it, surveys the troubled inward panorama of one's thoughts and feelings and shows what ought to be done.

For newcomers to the Quaker scene this may seem a risky internal operation. They feel that here is an invisible and intangible influence which would impose a powerful discipline on them and set them a standard to which they could never attain. They are not good enough to be Quakers.

This feeling cannot be disposed of just by saying that Quakers aren't saints. Of course they aren't: imperfection is part of the human condition. There is a serious psychological problem here which faces all people when a high ideal invades their hearts and begins to command their loyalty.

But it is not insoluble. You don't have to be a hero or a saint to follow the Quaker way, because you are not led into things that are beyond your powers. Although you may encounter great difficulties, they will not overcome you. You will find in practice that if the Quaker way is right for you, strength is given to follow it.

In the very difficult and dangerous circumstances in which they had to live, the early Friends were well aware of the need for that strength and the source from which it came. In the idiom and imagery of his time, George Fox wrote:

> Be still and cool in thy own mind and spirit from thy own thoughts, and then thou wilt feel the principle of God to turn thy mind to the Lord God, whereby thou wilt receive his strength and power from whence life comes, to allay all tempests, against blusterings and storms. That is it which moulds up into patience, into innocency, into soberness, into stillness, into stayedness, into quietness, up to God with his power.[34]

This was addressed to an individual, but the process Fox describes is strongly reinforced when people are together in Friends' meetings for worship. For most Friends there is an alternation between trying to live the Quaker way in the world - often with plenty of "blusterings and storms" - and the stillness and coolness of the gathered meeting. It isn't just that those present know that most of the others are in much the same case as themselves. They come to "know one another in the things that are eternal".[35] In that deep togetherness Quakers find strength to carry on in the face of difficulties, and comfort when the going is hard.

V

Quakers and the Arts

IN A QUAKER meeting there is no singing, and the meeting house has no stained glass windows or carvings. You may wonder whether this implies that there is no place for the arts in the Quaker way. This is not a side issue. You would be a very unusual person if you never listened to music or read a novel or went to the cinema or theatre or looked at a single painting. And it would not surprise me if you were more than merely a consumer of these arts but had tried your own hand at painting or pottery or writing verse or playing an instrument. The arts are a part of life and are woven into the fabric of practically all religions. No attempt to help you to explore the Quaker thing can therefore ignore them.

The attitude of Quakers to the arts is frankly puzzling and contradictory. The early Friends rejected all art - not merely the frivolous Restoration theatre or public amusements, but art of any kind, including serious art. There were no two ways about it. George Fox wrote that he was

> testifying against their Wakes and Feasts, their May-games, Sports, Play and Shows, which trained up People to Vanity and looseness.... I was moved to cry against all sorts of music, and against the Mountebanks playing tricks on their Stages, for they burdened the pure life, and stirred up people's minds to Vanity.[36]

At first there were exceptions, but this negative attitude soon hardened into a sort of orthodoxy. A classic case was that of Solomon Eccles, a distinguished composer, instrument maker and performer from a family of musicians. When he joined the Quakers he wrote a pamphlet against his own art, in which he said that "a Quaker.... being formerly of that Art, doth give his judgment and Sentence against it but yet approves of the Musick that pleaseth God". With Friends' tendency to put their ideas into practice, Solomon did not stop at words, but took his musical instruments to Tower Hill and set fire to them in public.[37]

Friends kept up this attitude into the present century, though as usual they were not quite monolithic about it. In the last fifty years, however, there has been a complete change. Many present-day Quakers enjoy the arts, and some are established professionals, including painters, novelists, playwrights, actors and entertainers.

It was firm evidence of this trend that about thirty years ago some Friends formed the Quaker Fellowship of the Arts to encourage and promote the idea that the arts could be a proper part of the Quaker way. At first QFA's efforts were looked at somewhat askance by some Friends, but it has now become an accepted part of the Quaker scene. It puts on art exhibitions and music recitals at Friend gatherings, and it has published the *Quaker Song Book.*

The real breakthrough came in 1978, when the Society's annual Swarthmore Lecture[36] entitled *Signs of Life* was delivered by Ormerod Greenwood, chair of QFA, a professional actor, producer and drama teacher. Another Swarthmore Lecture in 1984, entitled *The Two Cinnas,* was given by Laurence Lerner, Quaker poet and academic. The relationship between the Quaker way and the arts is explored in some detail in these two publications.

It is difficult to say what lies behind this radical change of attitude. Has the whole Quaker thing changed? So far as Friends' way of worship is concerned, obviously not. But Quakers have always had to live and work and practise the Quaker way in the world as it is. And the world in the second half of the 17th century was a very different world from the one we live in today. There had been a bitter civil war not many years before, one side of which consisted of people who were sternly opposed to all pleasures and believed that human beings are by nature sinful. Basically, Quakers did not share that outlook, but they had to live with the society into which they had been born. Perhaps they wanted to prove that they were after all earnest, solid citizens and not addicted either to frivolous amusement or to the eccentricities of the way-out sects which then abounded? But my guess is that they were motivated by something far deeper than political tactics. The whole business of art sat uneasily with what they had discovered in their own hearts, and in the prevailing climate of the time they failed to come to terms with that uneasiness.

But that still leaves the puzzle as to why it took them over 250 years to start trying to sort themselves out in this matter. Attempts at getting to the bottom of this problem would lead me into deeper waters than I can swim in; and I am well aware that writing about the meaning of art tends to be as boring as trying to explain a joke. All I can do here is to throw out a few thoughts which may be a starting point for more serious exploration.

Some main points about art

The following points seem to the lay person like myself to be inherent in the artistic process.

(1) Something drives artists to develop their skills to the highest level they can attain. A painter friend of mine used to call it "the urge". Wisely, he never tried to define it, for it is beyond words, as the Quaker thing is. Only by its products can you know that it is there.

(2) Real artists are trying to say something they desperately want others to hear, and serious consumers of art are trying, even if only subconsciously, to learn about themselves and the world. Between them, producer and consumer are seeing a little deeper into what life is about - at least they firmly believe they are. Some artists have succeeded so well in this that everyone recognises their work. The curves of the great sculptors set standards of beauty; the themes of the great composers lurk in the minds of ordinary people; the phrases of the great poets have become part of everyday speech.

(3) The consumers of art value the work of the producers so highly that they are prepared to pay for it. That may sound sordidly commercial, but willingness to pay is a rough-and-ready indicator that something that really matters is on offer. Even the ablest amateur is not valued quite as much as the artist who lives - or starves - on their art.

(4) There is a paradoxical element of satisfaction and enjoyment in the artistic process. Artists "scorn delights and live laborious days" to produce their work, and the consumers get pleasure from it and are often prepared to labour themselves to understand it. However apparently trivial the subject, artists put everything they have into it. A pair of comedians will work and work on an act until it seems about as funny to them as a lump of chewing gum.

(5) It is almost literally a matter of life and death to artists to resist restrictions or interference from any quarter. They claim to be carrying on a valid activity and have a right to portray the world as they see it.

(6) The themes of artistic work may be sordid, terrifying or disgusting, as well as beautiful and elevating. Tragedy is as "enjoyable" as comedy. Art often lays bare a fundamental opposition between two different levels of experience. Below the surface, in exalted states of delight or danger, the little pleasures and sorrows of everyday life seem trivial, but seen from the everyday standpoint the events of the grand cosmic plane of the artist can seem nonsensical or neurotic.

The collision between art and religion

It is mainly this last point that has given rise to difficulties with the Quaker thing. Artists' work takes them into a region of the human psyche which could easily be labelled "religious", but artists' basic attitude forbids them to take sides on matters of beliefs or morality. To a sincerely religious person, artistic activity can therefore seem amoral or even immoral; and those who play about with artistic skills can seem to be yielding to a perverse desire to pry into the secrets of the human condition without a serious thought for the Creator of it all. For artists who are religious in any serious sense, this feeling can set up a painful internal conflict. The early Friends can perhaps be forgiven for taking a tough line with themselves and rejecting art altogether.

A less heroic, but in practice more difficult, solution is for artists to dedicate their art wholly or mainly to religious themes - to the glory of God. Examples of artists who have done this are Bach in music, Blake in painting, and George Herbert and Gerard Manley Hopkins in literature. But the path of the well-meaning religious or propagandist artist is strewn with pitfalls. Devoting their art to please God, or to promote worthy moral, political or social causes can very easily have a bad effect on artists' performances *as* artists. For instance, if you turn over the pages of *Hymns Ancient and Modern* you will encounter much Christian theology skilfully and devotedly put into neat rhyming verses, but only here and there will you find real poetry. Compare number sixty-nine, the hymn which begins "Behold the great creator makes/ himself a house of clay/ A robe of virgin flesh he takes/ which he will wear for aye" with number sixty-seven, where the poetic genius of Christina Rossetti was at work. It begins "In the bleak midwinter/ Frosty wind made moan/ Earth stood hard as iron/ Water like a stone". Both hymns serve their purpose well, but artistically they inhabit different worlds. It is perhaps no accident that number 67 attracted a beautiful setting by Gustav Holst.

The American Quaker poet John Greenleaf Whittier got into difficulties when he wrote poems against slavery. They abound with morally impeccable lines like "Champion of those that groan beneath/ Oppression's iron hand", which even the kindest critic could hardly regard as poetry. But he was aware of the problem and wrote of himself: "he heard the fitful music still/ Of winds that out of dreamland blow". And when he listened to that music, he could square the circle by producing an image like "a dead fact stranded on the shore/ Of the oblivious years".

In *A Guide for the Perplexed*, E.F.Schumacher[39] perhaps goes some way towards resolving the issue. He says: "No great artist has ever turned his back on either entertainment or propaganda, or was ever satisfied with just these two. Invariably he strives to communicate truth, the power of truth, by appealing to man's higher intellectual faculties, which are supra-rational.... All great works of art are 'about God' in the sense of showing to the perplexed human being the path, the way up the mountain...." Art disposes us to wish to make the ascent, which is what we really want to do all the time, but keep forgetting.

In other words, art can be seen as part of a vision of wholeness, of an ideal of total spiritual, mental and physical health; another example of the sense of ultimate unity with the whole creation that is one outward sign of the Quaker thing. We can be helped towards that vision by both tragedy and comedy, because they both warn us about what happens when "Man's dominion/ has broken Nature's social union".[40]

Where do Quakers now stand?

The dilemma of the religious artist remains, and Quaker artists have to cope with it in a particularly acute form. They have to ask themselves: are the images that arise like a surge of sexual desire or a pain pleading for relief really something of the same kind as what happens in a Quaker meeting, where all images are put aside and it is dark and silent in the inward landscape? Can these be equally valid manifestations of that which is beyond all images?

This uneasy feeling is exacerbated by the strong moral element in the Quaker way of life. The Quaker thing illuminates Friends' egos and exerts a continuous and ever-present influence on their attitudes and conduct in every aspect of their personal and working lives, and they cannot escape from that gentle pressure. It keeps some people at a distance. In an article on "Why I am not a Friend", the writer Vera Brittain wrote, regretfully, "I have not found.... that by joining the Society of Friends a would-be artist can avoid becoming a less significant artist, in the endeavour to achieve the moral status of a social philanthropist."[41]

Quaker artists could of course follow Whittier's example and choose their subject matter accordingly. But if they are real artists they will be just as suspicious as any other artist of anything that might compete with the urge that drives them or might dictate how it shall function. Some of the Quaker artists I know discount the problem and say that they find no serious difficulty in combining their work as artists with their lives as Friends. They sometimes remind me that in the Quaker way the religious and the secular are not kept in watertight compartments. On the other hand, Laurence Lerner in the Swarthmore Lecture I have mentioned said, "I admire those Friends for whom all experience is a unity and who feel their love of literature is integrated into their Quakerism but I am not one of them."[42]

Friends as consumers of art, too, are exposed to the same internal conflicts as the producers, and it is too soon to be sure that they have fully resolved the conflict. The purely negative attitude of early Friends has certainly gone, but there is a danger of its being replaced by a state of mind that regards the arts as no more than a fairly harmless amusement - "as an amenity and not a necessity, with mild pleasure rather than passionate intensity, as a relief from life's pressures rather than a way of harnessing them." [43]

Unless I am mistaken, however, there is a pattern in the taste of Quakers. Significantly, perhaps, they seem to appreciate the works of artists who have combined their art with their religion. In music you can expect to find records of Bach, Bruckner and Vaughan Williams in Quaker homes; in painting Blake may be prominent; in poetry, Donne, Vaughan and other mystical poets. In meetings for worship, T.S.Eliot may be the poet who is most often quoted. You can't pinpoint what these artists have in common that attracts Friends; but the appeal seems unmistakably to be there. Perhaps equally significantly, Friends seem not to show the same predilection for Milton. Though, as always, I can immediately think of an exception.

As to Quaker producers of art, there has been little time for a pattern to develop, but when you encounter the sculpture of Peter Peri, the music of Tony Biggin, or the writings of Clive Sansom or

Reginald Reynolds or the novelist and playwright Alison Leonard, you can't help feeling that there is something in the tone of their work - their attitude to their subject-matter - which would not be there if they had not been Quakers. What that something is defies analysis or description, but if you are wondering whether the Quaker way is for you, it is a partial test to ask yourself whether you feel an affinity with the artists, great or minor, Quaker and non-Quaker, I have been referring to.

I must not leave this aspect of the Quaker way without mentioning an exciting development which has mushroomed since 1978, oddly enough in just those arts that the early Quakers so roundly condemned: drama and music.

It began with an amateur revue at the Society's Yearly Meeting in Lancaster during which Ormerod Greenwood's Swarthmore Lecture was delivered. This grew into a Quaker Youth Theatre company, The Leaveners, with some 150 members from 16-23 years of age. The members get together in different parts of the country to create music dramas, revues, and street theatre.

Since then there have been developments in other directions, such as the Quaker Festival Orchestra and Chorus which performs specially commissioned oratorios, and the Leaveners' Experiment in Arts for Peace (LEAP) which is a drama and conflict resolution project for unemployed young people. These projects are financed by Quaker charitable trusts, and have as their patrons the actors Paul Eddington, Ben Kingsley and Judi Dench, the songwriter Sydney Carter, and, in the past, the late Donald Swann and Gerald Priestland.

The underlying theme of many of these activities is peace and peacemaking, and the problem of marrying art with propaganda cannot be evaded. But the Quaker way is not working for one particular side or fighting for a cause; it sees all sides as part of a whole, and regards no cause as worth fighting for with outward weapons. So, in the main, it keeps in touch with the realities and complexities of life.

Here I must end these reflections. The significance of the arts is still not clear to Friends themselves, and perhaps never will be. One thing is clear: there is no danger of you being rejected by Friends for being a professional artist or taking a serious interest in the arts. If you feel like exploring this subject more deeply, I suggest that you start by reading the two Swarthmore Lectures I have referred to (they will be in the local Meeting House library) and then nobble a Friend artist or art-lover - as I have said there are quite a few of them around - and question him or her. You are not likely to solve the puzzles I have described, but you might learn quite a bit about the Quaker way.

VI
Fragment

The Quaker Thing in Science and Technology

EDITOR: *Frustratingly, the section on the Arts is the last part that Richard completed before his death. The section on Science and Technology remains in note form, and this is particularly irksome for the reader because Richard was himself a scientist, and could have provided us with many insights.*

His references include Michael Denton, Jacques Monod, Edward Thomas, Rupert Sheldrake and Richard Dawkins, as well as material of his own that he had earlier developed for talks to Friends on 'Evolutionism' and 'The Use and Abuses of Science'.

Some extracts will give the flavour:

What makes scientists, like artists, "scorn delights and live laborious days" to do work of this kind? First and foremost, they have an insatiable curiosity; second, a passionate desire to find out the cause of everything; third, a keen sensitivity to spot anything unusual which doesn't have an obvious known cause; fourth, an imaginative and creative turn of mind that gives rise to an endless flow of hypotheses as to the causes of observed events; fifth, an unwearying persistence in testing and verifying hypotheses. Finally, there is an overwhelming drive behind the whole exercise - an element of sheer joy in exercising skills and solving problems.

This joy can only be experienced to be understood. I began my own working life with three years as a scientific research worker. *(He notes elsewhere that he was then forced by family poverty to earn his living in other ways.)* I was never an outstanding performer, but after fifty years I could take you to the spot in Bushey Park near the Diana Fountain where I thought of a solution to an experimental problem that had defeated us in the laboratory and held up a useful piece of research for a year.... I had been studying something quite different during the evening and was in a tired but peaceful frame of mind when I went out for my walk before going to bed. As I was walking along enjoying the cool night air, the solution seemed to drop out of the sky, from nowhere. I turned on my heel and ran the whole mile back to my lodgings, seized a piece of paper, made a few calculations to show how my idea would work, and ran round to my immediate superior's house a quarter of a mile away and put the paper in his letter-box. When we met the following morning, we just looked at one another and got on with designing the apparatus required.

.... Does this in some way reflect the Quaker thing? The question cannot, on moral grounds alone, be evaded. Physicists developed the atomic bomb, chemists are producing poison gases, biologists are working on germ warfare. At least half the world's scientists are involved in preparations for war. The pollution of air, sea and land is also a by-product of scientific discovery and invention. Quaker scientists, on the whole, have not been directly responsible for these developments - they extend their conscientious objection to war into these areas - but they have taken their part in building up the general body of scientific knowledge and know-how which have made the developments possible.

..... There is a yearning in human beings to find an explanation of the great mysteries of life. What is the world like? What lies behind the surface? What is the point of the endless succession of birth, growth, decay and death in living nature? Why do our own lives contain such a strange, almost haphazard mixture of pleasure and pain, joy and sorrow, beauty and repulsion? What are we all on earth for? What is our place in it all - midway between the unimaginably vast spaces of the galaxies and the unimaginably small world of the subatomic particle?

END NOTES

[1] The term 'Quaker' and 'Friend' are practically interchangeable. The full title of the Quaker organisation is 'The Religious Society of Friends (Quakers).

[2] John Donne *Satire III*.

[3] T.S. Eliot, *Four Quartets, East Coker, II*.

[4] There is an excellent history of the Society of Friends, *Portrait in Grey*, by John Punshon, published by QHS 1984.

[5] Marcus Aurelius, *Reflections*. II. 17.

[6] *Christian Faith & Practice*, § III.

[7] T.S. Eliot, *The Dry Salvages V*.

[8] Matthew 18:201.

[12] Apart from *Honest to God*, John Robinson's *Truth is Two-Eyed* is a good example of his style.

[13] I.T. Ramsey, *Religious Language*, SCM Press 1973

[14] T.S. Eliot, *Burnt Norton*, Section V.

[15] *Quaker Faith & Practice*, 19.04.

[16] *Quaker Faith & Practice*, 19.07.

[17] *Quaker Faith & Practice*, 27.28.

[18] *ibid*. 27.27.

[19] *Quaker Faith & Practice*, 19.28.

[20] Luke 22:24.

[21] If you are of a theological turn of mind, you will find it interesting to read the Quaker response to the World Council of Churches 'Lima Text' on Baptism, Eucharist and Ministry, in the proceedings of London Yearly Meeting of the Society 1986. The book *To Lima with Love* is obtainable from Friends Book Centre. It is not so much what the response says as the style and approach that are significant.

[22] *Christian Faith & Practice,* § 129.

[23] Corinthians 13:12.

[24] *Quaker Faith & Practice,* 27.13.

[25] *Quaker Faith & Practice,* 19.28.

[26] *Quaker Faith & Practice,* 26.61.

[27] For a development of this thinking, you may like to read *Quaker Faith & Practice* 3.02-3.06 and 20.67-20.75.

[28] John Woolman, *The Journal and Essays,* ed. Gunmere, 1922, p 380.

[29] *Quaker Faith & Practice* 20.31.

[30] For further information, write to the William Allen Society, 4 Mercers Road, London N19 4PJ.

[31] Matthew 6:33-37.

[32] *Bringing the Invisible into the Light,* Quaker Home Service 1986.

[33] published by QHS 1964 (first published 1963), re-issued with an introduction 1990.

[34] *Quaker Faith & Practice* 2.18.

[35] *Advices & Queries* 18.

[36] For more on this topic see *Quaker Faith & Practice* 21.31.

[37] The quotations from George Fox and Solomon Eccles are from the 1978 lecture, pp 17 and 13 respectively. Both lectures and all other Quaker publications quoted here can be obtained from Friends Book Centre, Friends House, London NW1 2BJ.

[38] The Swarthmore Lecture was established in 1907 for 'some subject relating to the message and work' of the Society of Friends. The name was chosen in memory of the Cumbrian home of Margaret Fell (who, after the death of her husband Judge Fell, became the wife of George Fox), which served as headquarters for the budding Quaker movement.

[39] published by Jonathan Cape 1977, p143.

[40] Robert Burns, *To a Mouse, on turning up her nest with a plough, November 1785.*

[41] quoted in the 1978 Swarthmore Lecture, p56-7.

[42] 1984 Swarthmore Lecture, p57.

[43] 1978 Swarthmore Lecture, p57.

INDEX

Simplicity
Truth
Equality
Peace